Twayne's United States Authors Series

EDITOR OF THIS VOLUME

Sylvia E. Bowman
Indiana University

Hamlin Garland

TUSAS 299

Hamlin Garland

HAMLIN GARLAND

By JOSEPH B. McCULLOUGH

University of Nevada, Las Vegas

TWAYNE PUBLISHERS

A DIVISION OF G. K. HALL & CO., BOSTON

Library of Congress Cataloging in Publication Data

McCullough, Joseph B
  Hamlin Garland.

  (Twayne's United States authors series; TUSAS 299)
  Bibliography: p. 125 - 40
  Includes index.
  1.   Garland, Hamlin, 1860 - 1940 — Criticism and
interpretation.
PS1733.M27   813'.5'2   77-15002
ISBN 0-8057-7203-0

MANUFACTURED IN THE UNITED STATES OF AMERICA

For
My Children,
Roni, Joey, Stephanie and Tessie
and for
My Mother and Father

Contents

About the Author

Joseph B. McCullough is at present associate professor of English at the University of Nevada, Las Vegas, and acting dean of the Graduate College. A graduate of Gonzaga University, he took his M.A. and Ph.D. at Ohio University.

Dr. McCullough has edited, with Dr. Robert K. Dodge, a volume of contemporary Indian poetry entitled *Voices from Wah'kon-tah* (1974). He has also contributed articles on Mark Twain, Henry James, and Hamlin Garland to various professional journals, including *American Literature, American Literary Realism, Papers of the Bibliographical Society of America, Mark Twain Journal, Papers on Language and Literature, English Journal,* and *Pembroke Magazine.* He is presently at work on an edition of the letters of Hamlin Garland and on a volume of annotated criticism of Stephen Crane.

Preface

Hamlin Garland's place in the literary history of the United States has been assured by the historians of the past; for, during a productive and varied literary career, he published almost fifty volumes. But his reputation rests principally on his fiction written before 1895, and particularly on his volume of short stories, *Main-Travelled Roads*, and on his autobiography, *A Son of the Middle Border*. In those volumes, Garland demonstrated that it had at last become possible to deal with the American farmer in literature as a human being instead of seeing him simply through a veil of literary convention. By creating new types of characters, Garland hoped not only to inform readers about the realities of Western farm life but to touch the deeper feelings of a nation.

Unfortunately, Garland was seldom able to integrate his social and literary theories with the materials he gathered from personal experience and observation. Whenever Garland was able to maintain a tension between his romantic individualism and the oppressive social and economic conditions that threatened this individualism, his work retained a compelling vitality. But his literary achievements often fall short of our expectations. With the exception of *A Son of the Middle Border*, critics have almost unanimously disparaged Garland's work written after 1895. Yet, while Garland's best work was produced before 1895, the majority of his later work is by no means totally contemptible. In fact, scattered among it are some of his best pieces.

In this work I have been concerned with the aspects of Garland's life which influenced his writing. I have also examined his literary achievements in relation to his social and literary ideas. Finally, I have examined the major writings of each phase of Garland's literary career, which can be divided into three phases, although each phase contains elements from the others: an early period of involvement in reform movements and middle-border fiction (1888 - 1895); a period of Rocky Mountain romance (1896 - 1916); and a final phase of literary autobiography (1917 - 1940).

While I have used a modified chronological progression, I have only departed from it slightly to retain a thematic unity. Thus, after an initial biographical chapter, and one treating the development of Garland's literary theory, I have devoted separate chapters to Garland's middle-border fiction, to his economic fiction, his romantic Western fiction, and his autobiographical fiction. I have also included a separate chapter, "Toward Romanticism," which concerns the transition of Garland's work from his early realism to his later romanticism.

While I have attempted to describe the body of Garland's work and to treat individually as many works as possible, space has permitted only incidental notice of Garland's poetry, most of which is unsuccessful; of his essays, except those which directly influence his literary theory; and of some of his minor novels, such as those dealing with psychic phenemena. However, I have been careful not to exclude anything which would be necessary for an understanding of the major phases of Garland's literary career, or which, had they been included, would alter an interpretation or an estimation of his work.

I am indebted to Donald Pizer for his aid and suggestions during the early stages of this study and also for his permission to quote from his excellent study, *Hamlin Garland's Early Work and Career*, as well as to Robert Mane for his helpful suggestions. I am also indebted to Mrs. Constance Garland Doyle and Mrs. Isabel Garland Lord, who have kindly provided me with the photograph of Hamlin Garland and who have given me permission to quote from *A Son of the Middle Border*, *A Daughter of the Middle Border*, and *The Book of the American Indian*.

I wish to thank the University of Nevada, Las Vegas, for a grant for the preparation of the manuscript; Glenn W. Bundy, Curator, American Literature Collection, University of Southern California; and the librarians at the University of Nevada, Las Vegas, and the University of California at Berkeley. I particularly wish to thank Paula Tovey for her assistance in typing the manuscript. Also, I wish to thank Sylvia Bowman, whose helpful editorial comments have improved the text considerably. Finally, and most important, I am deeply grateful to Judy who taught me things and gave me qualities I could not learn from books.

JOSEPH B. McCULLOUGH

University of Nevada, Las Vegas

Chronology

1860   Hamlin Garland born September 14 near West Salem, Wisconsin.

1868   Family moves to Winneshiek County, Minnesota.

1869   Family moves to Dry Run, near Osage, Mitchell County, Iowa.

1876   Family moves to Osage where Garland entered Cedar Valley Seminary from which he graduated in June, 1881.

1881 -
1883   Travels and takes odd jobs; takes trip to the East with brother, Franklin; returns to the West, where he takes up a claim in McPherson County, South Dakota.

1884 -
1887   Goes to Boston in October, 1884; immerses himself in reading literature, as well as Charles Darwin, Herbert Spencer and John Fiske; reads Henry George's *Progress and Poverty;* teaches private classes in literature; lectures in and around Boston.

1887   Meets William Dean Howells; July - September, makes an extended visit to the West—Chicago, Osage, Ordway, Onalaska—to gather material for fiction; returns to Boston.

1891   Publishes *Main-Travelled Roads,* containing six stories of the Middle West; meets Stephen Crane; campaigns in Iowa for the Farmers' Alliance.

1892   A *Spoil of Office, Jason Edwards,* and A *Member of the Third House;* teaches at the Seaside Assembly, Avon by the Sea, New Jersey; campaigns in Iowa for the People's Party.

1893   Delivers a paper at the World's Columbian Exposition on "Local Color in Fiction"; settles in Chicago, making periodic trips to the East, South, and West.

1894   *Crumbling Idols.*

1895   *Rose of Dutcher's Coolly.*

1897   Takes a trip through the West, living on several Indian reservations.

1898   Returns to Washington, D.C., to complete Ulysses S. Grant project; leaves for a trip to Alaska; publishes *Ulysses S. Grant: His Life and Character.*

1899	Trip to England; marries Zulime Taft.
1900	Death of his mother; publishes *The Eagle's Heart*.
1902	*Captain of the Gray-Horse Troop*.
1903	*Hesper*.
1916	Moves to New York.
1917	*A Son of the Middle Border*.
1918	Elected to the American Academy of Arts and Letters.
1921	Publishes *A Daughter of the Middle Border*, for which he was awarded the Pulitzer Prize.
1923	*The Book of the American Indian*.
1930	Moves to Los Angeles.
1940	March 4, Garland dies.

CHAPTER 1

A Stranger on Parnassus

I Early Tensions

BORN on September 14, 1860, on a farm near West Salem,
Wisconsin, Hamlin Garland was the second of four children. His
father, Richard Garland, a native of Oxford County, Maine, quickly
became the dominant figure in his early life. Hamlin remembered
his father as a stern military disciplinarian who continually moved
his family westward—from certainty to uncertainty, from a modest
but comfortable home to a shanty—in search of a better life, and
who refused, despite setbacks, to "back trail," to retreat and accept
a life of ease.[1] Because of his father's domineering nature, Hamlin
was drawn to his mother, Isabelle McClintock Garland, who
accepted Richard's migratory nature with quiet resignation, despite
the suffering and the hardships of the moves. The contrast between
Garland's parents was to leave him with a particular tenderness
toward women — a tenderness which Garland transformed into a
recurring theme in which he dealt with suppressed and beaten farm
women.

When the Civil War came in 1861, Richard left his family to fight
for the Union; but he returned home in 1864. Restless and impatient, Richard moved his family to Winneshiek County, Minnesota, in 1868, and then to Mitchell County, Iowa, in August, 1869.
Again in the spring of 1876 the family was uprooted and was moved
to another farm near Osage, Iowa, because Richard had accepted
the position of wheat buyer for the Grange. In March, much to the
delight of Hamlin, who was not finding the hardships of farm life
very palatable, and his mother, the family moved into town.
However, the family moved back on the farm within a year.

II Early Years on the Farm

Garland's early years on the farm were difficult; he was expected
to do a man's work: plowing, sowing, threshing, cornhusking, hay-

13

ing, caring for the animals, and cleaning the stables. He recalled afterward that, after a day of "dragging," "you can scarcely limp home to supper, and it seems that you cannot possibly go on another day—but you do—at least I did."[2] He gradually developed an intense dislike for farm work and desired to escape to a better life. At this point, however, his aspirations were undirected: he only knew that he did not want to spend his life on the Middle Border—the prairie region that included Iowa, Minnesota, Wisconsin, Nebraska, and the Dakotas—which was an important agricultural frontier from about 1870 to 1900.

In 1876, Hamlin was allowed to enroll in Cedar Valley Seminary; but he spent only half of the year in school; for he returned to the farm each spring to help with the planting and harvesting until his graduation in 1881. As his aversion to work increased, he was inclined to rebel against being forced to return each year to help on the farm, but he felt equally guilty about leaving his mother alone on the farm. While farm life did not allow for extensive reading, Garland's first introduction to literature came at school through the McGuffey Reader where he "discovered" John Milton and William Shakespeare, and then Nathaniel Hawthorne and Victor Hugo. In addition to his reading, he developed an ambition to excel in oratory; and, although his father never understood his inclinations, his mother encouraged Hamlin to pursue and develop his talents. With a new intellectual life beginning to open, Garland's rebellion against his father and the farm increased. Upon graduation from the seminary in June, 1881, he left home for the first time to travel in the East where, during the next two years, he held a variety of odd jobs. He subsequently returned to South Dakota where his family had moved in 1881; but he left shortly afterward to teach school for a year in Illinois. He again returned to Dakota in the spring of 1883 to stake a claim, but he had no intention of remaining on the farm. He dreamed of a career in the East.

III   *Boston (1884)*

Although Garland had only a vague idea of what he wanted in the East, he made the most crucial decision in both his personal and artistic career in the fall of 1884. Possessing approximately one hundred and thirty dollars which remained from the sale of his claim and some letters of introduction (which finally proved to be useless) from a traveling minister named Brashford, he journeyed to Boston, the intellectual and literary center of the country.

By the time Garland arrived in Boston, he was already familiar with Hippolyte Taine and Robert Ingersoll. While in Boston, he eagerly read Walt Whitman's poetry; and he absorbed the poet's view of the spiritual brotherhood of workers as well as much of his nationalistic feeling. He also studied Charles Darwin, Herbert Spencer, John Fiske, Hermann Helmholtz, and Ernst Heinrich Haeckel in an effort to understand not only how evolutionary and biological processes in nature led from simple to complex forms but also how these processes could be applied to society. Particularly captivated by Spencer, he remarked that

Herbert Spencer remained my philosopher and master. With eager haste I sought to compass the "Synthetic Philosophy." The universe took on order and harmony. . . . It was thrilling, it was joyful to perceive that everything moved from the simple to the complex—how the bowstring became the harp, and the egg the chicken. . . . While my body softened and my muscles wasted from disuse, I skittered from pole to pole of the intellectual universe like an impatient bat. I learned a little of everything and nothing very thoroughly. With so many peaks in sight, I had no time to spend digging up the valley soil.[3]

Garland's reading of Henry George's *Progress and Poverty* in early 1884 confirmed his own experiences of farm life and quickly converted him into an advocate of the single tax which sought to correct the injustice of the unearned increment that favored property owners at the expense of the laboring farmer. As Donald Pizer suggests, it is possible to see a basic cast of mind revealed in Garland's choice of what to believe and accept in the years before his arrival in Boston, a cast of mind which helps explain the Garland of the years 1884 to 1895: "He was eager for the new truth, the new hope, which science offered as a substitute for what he called superstition. He preferred to see this new truth in two patterns. First, he wanted to explain complex social and intellectual problems by means of a readily graspable formula or key. Second, he wanted an explanation that conceived of the past as dead and benighted, of his own age as the crucial one, and of the future as bright with material and intellectual accomplishment and progress."[4] Involved with the intellectual and philosophical currents of the time, Garland desired to participate in them; but he had not the vaguest idea about where such involvement would take him. He simply felt that Boston somehow held the key to his success.

But, contrary to the ideal of Boston which Garland had formed in his mind, his first few months there were hardly more comfortable than the drudgery of the farm life that he had left. Seeing his struggle in almost epic terms, Garland later remarked that "No Jason ever sought a Golden Fleece with less knowledge of the sea before him. All waters were to me unchartered. It is impossible that any young man of to-day could be so ignorant and so venturesome, for I was utterly without help in time of trouble."[5] In order to make what little money he had last, he lodged in a dingy room in Boylston Place near the public library. His meals consisted of barely enough to survive; he walked everywhere he went; and he generally attended only those lectures and concerts which were free.[6] When he timidly ventured to Harvard University to see if he could attend lectures, he was abruptly told that there was no place for outside students. In order to even check out books at the public library, Garland needed an endorsement because he was neither a student nor an employee of a local business. When he boldly decided to visit Edward Everett Hale, one of the directors of the library, at his home, Hale, impressed with Garland's enthusiasm, gave Garland the proper letters to help him secure a library card and thus became the first in a long series of acquaintances who encouraged him and did not treat him like an "outsider."

During the first winter in Boston, the only extravagance which Garland permitted himself was attending paid performances of Shakespeare's plays by the noted actor, Edwin Booth. Since his early school days in Cedar Valley, Garland had fancied himself as an orator; but, as he once said, "Edwin Booth taught me the power and the glory of English Speech. He made me feel very rude and small and poor, but he inspired me. He aroused my ambition."[7] From this renewed interest in oratory, he then attended a lecture by Moses True Brown, the principal of the Boston School of Oratory. After these two men became acquainted, Brown offered to allow Garland to attend school free of charge but in exchange for Garland's comments on one of Brown's manuscripts for a book. Later, Garland was approached by Mrs. Payson, a student at the school, to give three lectures about Victor Hugo, Edwin Booth, and modern German and American novels. Although his lectures were well received, his money was nearly exhausted. Again Brown rescued him, this time by asking him to give a series of lectures. In January, 1886, Garland organized a class in American literature at the school. Through his lectures he met and became friends with Charles Hurd, the literary editor of the *Boston Evening Transcript;* and through him Garland initially found his way into print.

IV *Howells and Kirkland*

Although there are discrepancies in Garland's own dating, he met William Dean Howells sometime in mid-1887 in Boston. Although he had been critical of Howells in his lectures prior to 1886, he had not fully understood Howells' critical position. By 1887 Garland was an avid disciple of Howells, the reigning dean of American letters; and their meeting set the stage for a lifelong friendship which proved profitable both personally and artistically for Garland.

While the dominant trend in American literature before the Civil War was romantic, the widespread social, philosophical, and literary changes which occurred after the war shifted the emphasis to realism and then to naturalism. The change had been introduced by the local colorists, but the espousal of realism by Howells, Henry James, and Mark Twain gave the movement its impetus. Garland assumed the battle for local color.

When Garland reviewed Joseph Kirkland's *Zury: The Meanest Man in Spring County* in May, 1887, and considered it "The most realistic novel of American interior society yet written,"[8] he was calling attention to the trend in literature and, at the same time, making an implicit judgment about the responsibilities of the writer in America. He continued in the review that "The full realization of the inexhaustible wealth of native American material . . . will come to the Eastern reader with the reading of *Zury*. It is as native to Illinois as Tolstoy's *Anna Karenina* and Torguenieft's [*sic*] *Fathers and Sons* are to Russia, its descriptions are so infused with life and so graphic. The book is absolutely unconventional—not a trace of old-world literature or society—and every character is new and native."[9] Because of the favorable review, a correspondence ensued between the two men; and Garland, while on a trip to the West, stopped in Chicago on July 2, 1887, to see Kirkland.

V *A Return to the West*

In July, when Garland returned to the West, he did so in the first of a series of visits to gather material for his fiction. After having spent three years in the East, the barrenness of farm life had made a deeper impression on him than ever before. Garland remarked that "Something deep and resonant vibrated within my brain as I looked out upon this monotonous commonplace landscape. I realized for the first time that the east had surfeited me with picturesqueness. It appeared that I had been living for six years amid painted, neatly arranged pasteboard scenery. Now suddenly I dropped to the level of nature unadorned, down to the ugly unkempt lanes I knew so well, back to the pungent realities of the streamless plain."[10]

Even though Garland was aware of the essential tragedy and hopelessness of most middle-border life, he did not yet know that life in that region would be his story to tell.[11] But he was encouraged to do so by Joseph Kirkland who called Garland in a letter "the first actual farmer in American literature—now tell the truth about it."[12] Thus it was that by 1887 Garland had resolved to write fiction and had found his theme. He intended to interpret his section of the country to those readers who had no personal knowledge of, or exposure to, life on the middle border.

VI   *The Years of Authorship*

At the same time, however, Garland began to develop his strong sense of guilt aboout leaving his family, especially his mother, in such barren surroundings; yet he also knew that he would not remain on the farm, since his success as an artist dictated his return to the East. This conflicting tension, only one of many which Garland experienced during his career, was also to become a recurring theme in much of his fiction. Although Garland had published articles dealing with local color as early as 1885, he began taking copious notes about farm life during this 1887 trip. His second visit to the West in 1888, when his mother had suffered a stroke and was partially paralyzed, provided the stimulus for his resolution to write fiction.

Since he had also become a confirmed advocate of the single tax upon his return to Boston in the fall of 1887, he began contemplating how to use the doctrine in his fiction. Several of Garland's stories which were conceived during his trips to the West in 1887 and 1888, such as "A Common Case," "John Boyle's Conclusion," and "A Prairie Heroine," in addition to later stories such as "Under the Lion's Paw," indicate not only that Garland was sympathetic to the farmers but that he was clearly bitter about and resentful of the socioeconomic injustices of the land system.

At the same time Garland wrote a series of articles called "Boy Life on the Prairie" that described, autobiographically, farm life from the point of view of a boy in the 1870s. The six articles, published in 1888, later became part of *Boy Life on the Prairie*

(1899). These articles, together with such stories as "Daddy Deering" and "An Evening at the Corner Grocery," were drawn from his early experiences of growing up on the farm. As Donald Pizer suggests, "the predominant tone of almost every story was determined by what may be called Garland's chronology of vision—whether he was viewing the West as he recalled it from his boyhood or as he reacted against it in terms of adult ideas. . . . He had discovered two ways of viewing the west which involved him emotionally. One was to see it in terms of his social theories. The other was to see it through a reminiscent haze. In either case he had discovered his material and his themes."[13]

But between 1888 and 1890 Garland experienced difficulty in getting his material published. Finally, in 1889, his story "A Spring Romance" was accepted for publication by Richard Watson Gilder, the editor of the prestigious *Century*. Garland was elated to have the recognition and exposure of this leading magazine; but, since the *Century* was genteel and would only print Garland's milder material, it rejected anything which smacked of polemics. In addition, Gilder was slow about putting the material into print after it had been accepted; and, since Garland was eager to have his work printed, it was with considerable joy that he became acquainted with Benjamin O. Flower, the editor of the radical but widely read new journal, the *Arena*. Early in 1890 Flower accepted for publication Garland's story, "A Prairie Heroine," the bitter story about a broken farm wife which had earlier been rejected by Gilder. Flower then wrote to Garland:

I notice you have seemed to suppress your thoughts in two or three instances and have erased some lines from your story. In writing for the *Arena* either stories or essays I wish you always to feel yourself thoroughly free to express any opinion you desire or to send home any lessons you feel should be impressed upon the people. I for one do not believe in mincing matters when we are dealing with the great wrongs and evils of the day and the pitiful conditions of society and I do not wish you to feel in writing for the *Arena* at any time the slightest restraint.[14]

The *Arena* thus became Garland's most important literary outlet, and for more than two years he had an article in nearly every issue. He also immediately sent Flower his single-tax play, *Under the Wheel*, which Gilder had also rejected. In 1891, Flower further suggested that Garland collect some of his stories into a single volume; thus in June, 1891, *Main-Travelled Roads* appeared. In ad-

dition to these writings of the early 1890s, Garland lectured on
Henry George's theories; and, after the People's Party (Populists)
had been formed, he campaigned in Iowa in 1892 for the party's
candidates.

In August, 1891, Garland made a brief trip to Avon-by-the-Sea
where he presented a series of lectures,[15] and where he met Stephen
Crane, the journalist covering the lecture. As *Main-Travelled Roads*
had already appeared, Crane was interested in knowing more about
Garland. When Garland returned to Avon in August, 1892, he again
met Crane; but Crane was soon and abruptly fired from his job at
the *Tribune* because of his August 21 article "On the New Jersey
Coast," which had unkindly and ironically depicted an American
Day Parade of members of the United American Mechanics in
Asbury Park. Crane moved to New York; Garland undertook a trip
to the West Coast; the two did not keep in close touch; but Garland
was so impressed with Crane's *Maggie*, which he reviewed in 1893,
that he convinced Crane to send a copy to Howells; and this suggestion helped launch Crane's literary career.

Though Garland was appearing in print often by 1892, and was
also keeping busy lecturing and campaigning, Garland's work was
not selling as well as he had hoped. Furthermore, much of his
material was being criticized in both the East and the West. As
Garland recalled,

I had the foolish notion that the literary folk of the west would take local
pride in the color of my work, and to find myself execrated by nearly every
critic as "a bird willing to foul his own nest" was an amazement. Editorials
and criticisms poured into the office, all written to prove that my pictures of
the middle border were utterly false.

Statistics were employed to show that pianos and Brussels carpets adorn-
ed almost every Iowa farmhouse. Tilling the prairie soil was declared to be
"the noblest vocation in the world, not in the least like the pictures this
eastern author has drawn of it."[16]

Moreover, it became evident that the contrasting positions about
literary art espoused by Gilder and Flower provided a tension
within Garland. Garland not only wanted to tell the truth about life
on the middle border, and hopefully help change conditions, but
also desired the recognition and the success as an artist that the
praise and respect by Gilder would give him. Flower was Garland's
social and ethical conscience, but Gilder was his aesthetic conscience. Fundamentally, Garland's was a struggle to identify his ar-

tistic mission which in one form or another troubled him for the rest of his life. His simplicity of existence on the farm had become complicated by compelling responsibilities to society which he felt he must assume; yet he had a strong personal need to be accepted and successful as an artist.

As Garland traveled during 1892 participating in the Populist revolt, he was becoming increasingly aware of changes occurring in farm life. He mentions that,

After nearly a third of a century of migration, the Garlands were about to double back on their trail, and their decision was deeply significant. It meant that a certain phase of American pioneering had ended, that "the woods and prairie lands" having all been taken up, nothing remained but the semiarid valley of the Rocky Mountains. "Irrigation" was a new word and a vague word in the ears of my father's generation, and had little of the charm which lay in the "flowery savannahs" of the Mississippi Valley. In the years between 1865 and 1892 the nation had swiftly passed through the buoyant era of free land settlement, and now the day of reckoning had come.[17]

In early 1893 Garland convinced his parents to move from their Dakota farm and resettle in West Salem; he decided to leave Boston and reside in Chicago. Establishing himself with the new but respectable publishing house of Herbert S. Stone and Hannibal I. Kimball, who were his publishers until 1896 when the firm dissolved, he began drifting away from the more radical Benjamin O. Flower and the *Arena*.

Besides his literary manifesto, *Crumbling Idols*, which appeared in 1894, the most significant work that Garland published while in Chicago was *Rose of Dutcher's Coolly*, which he wrote during 1893 and 1894 before it finally appeared in 1895. Despite the fact that this was his most ambitious and probably his best novel, Garland was depressed at its poor reception; for the novel was brutally attacked for its sexual themes. Yet, even while working on *Rose*, he had begun meditating on themes connected with the Far West.[18]

Garland began making more frequent trips to the West, and was delighted that his early attempts at fiction dealing with the "high country" had a wide appeal. The final blow to his reform spirit occurred when the Populist Party was defeated by William McKinley in 1896. Thereafter Garland shifted the locale for his stories to the Rocky Mountain area. Furthermore, his fiction became much more romantic, even though romance and sentimentality had never been

wholly absent from his earlier material. Indeed, a commonplace in
Garland criticism is the attempt to explain or justify Garland's
"decline from realism" after 1895.[19] However, most of the views,
though providing some insight, tend to see his shift as more radical
than it really was; they fail to distinguish between Garland's expressed intent in his earlier material and his achievement.

As Donald Pizer perceptively indicates, "The emotional center of
reference of Garland's thought . . . was the romantic individualism
characteristic of the major segment of the nineteenth-century
American mind. . . . And because the freedom of the individual is
perenially being oppressed or threatened or ignored, Garland was a
radical, a reformer, just as Emerson and Whitman were in the same
sense reformers and radicals in their attempts to state and to advocate individualistic philosophies."[20] Garland himself attempted to
explain his interest and his shift in locale:

All my emotional relationships with the "High Country" were pleasant, my
sense of responsibility was less keen, hence the notes of resentment, of opposition to unjust social conditions which had made my other books an
offense to my readers were almost entirely absent in my studies of the
mountaineers. My pity was less challanged in their case. Lonely as their
lives were, it was not a sordid loneliness. The cattle rancher was at least not
a drudge. Careless, slovenly and wasteful as I knew him to be, he was not
mean. He had something of the Centaur in his bearing. Marvelous
horsemanship dignified his lean figure and lent a notable grace to his
gestures. His speech was picturesque and his observations covered a wide
area. Self-reliant, fearless, instant action in emergency, his character
appealed to me with ever-increasing power.[21]

Garland was becoming impatient with Stone and Kimball's, for
his material was not selling as well as he had anticipated. The sales
from *Rose of Dutcher's Coolly* were poor; but Harold Frederick's
The Damnation of Theron Ware, which was published by Kimball
in 1896 and which was equally shocking to the critics, immediately
sold twenty thousand volumes. However, in 1896 Kimball signed a
two-year contract for publication rights on *Prairie Folks* and
Crumbling Idols. At the same time, Garland finalized an agreement
with McClure's to publish a series of installments on Ulysses S.
Grant.[22]

Garland moved to Washington, D.C., in order to have more time
for the Grant project, but he became dissatisfied with the way that
McClure's was handling his material, primarily the drastic cutting

his manuscript received by the editors. He suspected that their reasons were more financial than literary. In early 1897, he began to lean toward D. Appleton & Company as his chief publisher; and in February, 1897, he signed a contract with that publisher, providing for a straight fifteen percent royalty, for *A Spoil of Office* (which was released by Stone & Kimball), and for a new volume of stories to be called *Wayside Courtships*. Garland published several installments of the Grant project, but McClure's finally quit publishing what had originally been contemplated as a full-length study.[23] With the Grant study in abeyance, Garland turned to the West in 1897.

He stopped by West Salem to meet his brother, Franklin, and there outlined a tour which would begin with a study of the Sioux at Standing Rock Reservation in North Dakota and end at Seattle and the Pacific Ocean. With letters of introduction from General Nelson A. Miles, and accompanied by Ernest Thompson Seton, the Garlands left for Standing Rock. For the next month Hamlin lived among the Sioux, Crow, and Cheyenne Indians. His observations were the basis of many stories, essays, and a novel. As Garland later remembered, "To me this was a thrilling glimpse into prehistoric America, for these young men, stripped of their tainted white-rags, were wholly admirable, painted lithe-limbed warriors, rejoicing once again in the light of their ancestral moons. On every face was a look like that of a captive leopard, dreaming of far-seen, familiar sands. The present was forgot, the past was momentarily restored."[24]

When the brothers reached the end of their proposed trip, Hamlin became so excited about the news of the Yukon gold strike that he was ready to depart immediately for Alaska. However, he decided to postpone the trip temporarily in order to return to Washington to finish his Grant biography. As soon as this literary project was completed, and against the protestations of his friends and family, he set out for the Yukon in 1898, a trip which he recounted in *The Trail of the Goldseekers* (1899). As Jean Holloway suggests, the motivation for this trip was more complicated than Garland's craving for adventure and sudden wealth or than his love of the outdoors. As his future course was uncertain, he was turning more and more to thoughts of his origin, to nostalgia for the simpler conditions of his boyhood. But, however vivid his memoirs, the Middle West of his youth had disappeared; and the unoccupied lands of Colorado and the Northwest reminded him of the land of

his youth.[25] As Garland himself remarked, "It was like going back to
the prairies of Indiana, Illinois and Iowa, as they were sixty years
ago, except in this case the elk and deer were absent."[26]

A few days after his return from the Yukon in September, 1898,
Garland was given an advance copy of *Ulysses S. Grant, His Life
and Character*. Despite the difficulties he had encountered with
McClure's in the early stages of the study, he was happy with the
final product. In fact, he maintained to the end of his life that it was
one of his best books.[27] Garland left Washington for a prolonged
visit with his parents before returning to Chicago, where he renewed several artistic acquaintances and where he planned a trip to
England, which was to be the first of several for him. When he
arrived in London, he was conscious of the fact that he was at both
personal and artistic crossroads. He later characterized the conflict
between "genteelism" and "bohemianism" in terms of clothes. He
felt that to continue his present course "would be to have as ex-
amplars Walt Whitman, Joaquin Miller, John Burroughs and other
illustrious non-conformists to whom long beards, easy collars, and
short coats were natural and becoming. To take the other road was
to follow [James Russell] Lowell and [Edmund C.] Stedman and
Howells."[28]

Appropriately, Garland adopted the dress of London society; for
it symbolized the direction which his fiction was already taking.
Faced with much the same conflict as Mark Twain, who was attracted by genteel culture but who continued to resist it, Garland
was attracted by London high society. Of course, we may easily ex-
aggerate Garland's bohemianism, for he was never as unconventional as he would have us believe before this excursion. But for
Garland this trip was merely "another indication that the customs of
the Border were fading to memory, and that western society, which
had long been dominated by the stately figures of the minister and
the judge, was on its way to adopting the manners and customs of
the openly-derided but secretly admired 'four hundred.' "[29] He was
excited to meet James Barrie, Bret Harte, Sir Walter Besant,
Thomas Hardy, George Bernard Shaw, and Arthur Conan Doyle;
but the highlight of his trip was his invitation to attend the Authors'
Society Dinner.

It was only appropriate that, after his return from London,
Garland married Zulime Taft, sister of the famous sculptor Lorado
Taft; for she represented the respectability which he had already
accepted in principle. After his marriage, Garland honeymooned for

a brief time in the West before settling down at his desk in West Salem to write. He began to deluge Gilder with manuscripts which dealt with Western material, and he also began to write *The Captain of the Grey-Horse Troop* which reflected his active interest in the American Indian.

In November, 1900, the Garlands left for New York, where they planned to spend the winter; but Hamlin was urgently called back to West Salem because of his mother's approaching death. Her death, which came before his arrival, affected him deeply; for, as we have observed, had always had a strong attraction to his mother; he constantly sought her encouragement; he felt guilty for having left her alone on the farm; and he was resentful of his father for the difficult life she had been forced to lead. Even Garland's search for a bride had been influenced largely by her desire to have a "new daughter," and his mother's difficult life on the farm was probably responsible for Garland's determined fight for women's rights, as well as for his continual depiction of the tragic, unfulfilled, deprived life of the prairie woman. Garland briefly submerged his grief over his mother's death by writing a memorial story, "The Wife of a Pioneer."

Garland returned to Chicago, which was his permanent home until 1916, although he made frequent trips to the Far West, West Salem, and New York. He began to work intensely on his novel *The Captain of the Grey-Horse Troop*, which was finally published in 1902, and which was not only financially successful but also well received by the critics. Since Garland retained an interest in the Indian for many years, he wrote stories about them which he later collected in *Book of the American Indian*. In fact, President Theodore Roosevelt solicited Garland's advice about Indian affairs as a result of Garland's direct experience and understanding of Indian problems.

Garland's next literary project, however, dealt with physic experimentation—a relatively new and controversial field, but one which Garland had displayed an interest in as early as the 1890s. Despite well-publicized deceptions by many spiritualists, there remained in both England and America a group of enthusiasts dedicated to the investigation of psychic phenomena. In Boston one of the leaders of the movement, Minot J. Savage, continued to report his experiences with seances in the *Arena*. In 1891 at the suggestion of B. O. Flower, also a mystic, the American Psychical Society was formed with the appointment of the Reverend Ernest

Allen as secretary. Flower intended that the organization would do something in the way of experimental research on psychic phenomena and later publish the results in a journal. To give the organization the scientific viewpoint necessary for scientific investigation, Flower also recommended that three skeptics be enrolled as officers in the society: Amos E. Dolbear, physics professor at Tufts College; Rabbi Solomon Schindler; and Garland who, as a disciple of Darwin and Spencer, seemed to qualify as a member to provide the desired scientific balance.

As Garland traveled around the country in the early 1890s speaking for the Farmers' Alliance and gathering material for his middle-border fiction, he also attended many seances, reporting the results of what he saw to the society. But, since he was more interested in being known as a fiction writer and historian than as an advocate of psychic research, which was only a subsidiary interest, he simply compiled notes and recorded impressions with the intention to write, sometime, a novel with mediumship as its main theme.

In 1905 he finally published *Tyranny in the Dark*, a psychic novel which aroused some controversary. The story concerns the development of Viola Lambert whose parents, having discovered her mediumistic powers, use her as an instrument of communication between the living and the dead, and deny her the companionship and recreations natural to childhood. She is forced to endure long hours in the dark, surrounded by people who had little regard for her pain and disgust at being a slave to her powers.

Throughout the novel Garland was able to summarize the arguments for and against the validity of psychic phenomena, without appearing to take a definite stand himself. Rather, he was more interested in developing the theme of bondage to a cause, which he had discovered in all the mediums he had studied. He believed that whether they felt that it was their duty to sacrifice themselves or whether instead they employed their powers as a source of revenue, wherever they went they were forced to "demonstrate" their work and their "powers" were the only point of conversation. Slowly they lost the normal balance of body and mind, were no longer free agents, and in some cases went mad.

Garland continued to treat the subject of psychic phenomena in two more novels, *The Shadow World* (1908) and *Victor Olnee's Discipline* (1911). In the latter work, which was written as a sequel to *Tyranny in the Dark*, Garland seemed convinced of the supernatural quality of psychic experiences. However, it was generally damned by reviewers as "spiritualistic propaganda." Although Garland retained an abiding interest in the subject of psychic phenomena for the rest of his life, he was to give it very little attention in his remaining fiction.

In 1906, when Garland made his second trip to England, he covered much the same ground that he had on his first trip in 1899; and he paid special visits to Shaw, Israel Zangwill, Conan Doyle, and Rudyard Kipling. When he returned, his writing began to lag, although he still continued to promote various literary activities. In particular, he aided in the formation of "The Cliff Dwellers" Club in Chicago, named after Henry Fuller's novel, and was subsequently elected the club's first president.

In 1909 - 1910 Garland consolidated his literary properties. As his contract with Macmillan and Company had expired, he was allowed to purchase the plates of five volumes at one-half their cost. He then turned to Harper and Brothers as his new publishers. But, despite the change, his writing was going through a period of sterility. In 1913, physically ill and mentally weary, Garland found that he was unable to prepare new materials for his fiction.[30] He decided, therefore, in 1916 to move to New York to be closer to the publishers; he hoped to repeat the success he had found with *Boy Life on the Prairie* in 1899; for, if he could not create new material out of the present, he would re-create the past. In 1917, when *A Son of the Middle Border* appeared, Garland had begun the final phase of his literary career.

Prior to this work, Garland's fiction was never entirely without autobiographical elements; but the instant success of *A Son of the Middle Border*, which he had first sketched in *Boy Life*, influenced his decision to devote himself almost exclusively to this genre for the rest of his life. As Holloway suggests, "the temper of the times was a contributing factor to the favorable reception of a work which understandably had intrinsic merits. The wave of patriotism engendered by our belated entrance into the European conflict had turned attention to the national heritage. Historical volumes and reminiscent sidelights upon distinctive American characteristics found favor with the public."[31] And this genre also gave Garland the opportunity to investigate his own heritage, to evoke at times nostalgically the qualities of an America which had disappeared, and at other times to capture the inherent tragedy of the farmer on the middle-border.

In recognition of his achievement in *A Son of the Middle Border*

Garland, much to his delight, was elected to the American Academy of Arts and Letters. For Garland, the appointment climaxed the long road to literary acceptance. But the organization had its detractors, such as Irving Bacheller, who attacked the academy as undemocratic. Garland defended it, however, arguing that

My position is that of an intellectual aristocrat; I have no confidence in a "democratic art," if by that phrase is meant an art based on popular approval. With due regard for the welfare of the average man, I do not value his judgment upon wall-paper or rugs or paintings. Why should his verdict on a book or a play be considered something mystically sure and high and final? The Tolstoyan belief in "the intuitive rightness" of the peasant has always affected me as sentimental nonsense. I am gratified when my work appeals to a large number of my fellow republicans, but if one of my books were to have a very wide sale, I should at once lose confidence in its quality. The judgment of millions, when it comes to a question of art, is usually wrong.[32]

It is somewhat ironic that Garland espoused so firmly at this time his position relative to aristocratic art, because he had just gained the public approval which he had so desired when the public had rejected his earlier middle-border fiction. Had he maintained his earliest literary interests after the 1890s, he might have continued to develop his more realistic fiction which, while not gaining public approval, was of a much higher quality than his later, more romantic material.

In any event, Garland became absorbed with autobiography. In 1921, *Daughter of the Middle Border* appeared, for which he was given the Pulitzer Prize for biography. Garland wrote two more volumes of family autobiography, *Trail Makers of the Middle Border* (1926) and *Back-Trailers from the Middle Border* (1928), before moving to Los Angeles where he remained until his death on March 4, 1940. While in California, he reviewed the same material that he covered in his autobiographies, but he presented the material with a literary point of view in four more volumes: *Roadside Meetings, Companions on the Trail, My Friendly Contemporaries*, and *Afternoon Neighbors*. He also briefly revived his interest in the psychic world with *Forty Years of Psychic Research* (1936)—in which he reported upon his lifetime of experimentation with the occult, including his encounters with mediums and clairvoyants—and *Mystery of Buried Cross* (1939).

To argue that Garland's public acceptance was gained merely at the price of compromise is to ignore the complex formation of his basic cast of mind and his personal struggle to identify his artistic mission. But his enthusiastic acceptance of his election to the American Academy of Arts and Letters illustrates that Garland was no longer the "stranger on Parnassus" that H. L. Mencken once termed him.[33] Garland's surrender to conventional society—which he had described on his trip to England years earlier—had received a satiric, albeit gentle, treatment from his close friend, Henry B. Fuller, in "The Downfall of Abner Joyce" (1901). Detailing the many factors which aided in bringing about Abner's (Hamlin's) downfall that had culminated in his symbolic acceptance of his genteel wife and his evening dress, Fuller concluded in a passage which had an unfortunate ring of truth to it:

Yes, Abner had brought down, one after another, all the pillars of the temple. But he had dealt out his own fate along with the fate of the rest: crushed yet complacent, he lay among the ruins. The glamour of success and of association with the successful was dazzling him. The pomp and luxury of plutocracy inwrapped him, and he had a sudden sweet shuddering vision of himself dining with still others of the wealthy just because they *were* wealthy, and prominent, and successful. Yes, Abner had made his compromise with the world. He had conformed. He had reached an understanding with the children of Mammon. He—a great, original genius—had become just like other people. His downfall was complete.[34]

CHAPTER 2

Development of a Literary Creed

I *Influences*

Crumbling Idols, published in 1894, was Hamlin Garland's only major contribution to literary theory; but it marked the culmination in the evolution of his ideas which had occupied his attention from the time he had entered Boston nearly a decade earlier. Through his reading and his professional associations, he was involved in the extensive critical debates over realism and the nature of American literature. Though the sources of Garland's ideas are relatively complicated ones and his applications of the ideas are occasionally simplistic, he vigorously clung to the belief that local color should be the dominant form in American literature.

In general, the dominant trend in American literature before 1860 was romantic. But the vast social, economic, literary, and religious changes brought about by the Civil War and the new philosophies of life influenced by the advance of science had dispelled assumptions underlying romanticism. The result, a gradual shift from romanticism to realism and naturalism, was due mainly to the espousal of realism by Mark Twain, Henry James, and William Dean Howells; but the switch had been introduced by the local colorists who sought to present life more truthfully by presenting the facts of the immediate present. They attempted to reproduce the texture and background of life which they had personally experienced, and they observed American life in order to produce a national literature through national character.

Most realists followed Howells who had formulated a theory of art which included the use of the commonplace; who had advocated that character was more important than plot; and who in an attack on romanticism, had implied that realism was the true expression of democracy. He defined realism as "nothing more and nothing less than the truthful treatment of material";[1] but he also argued that, while writers should maintain in their works a fidelity to experience

30

and not romanticize the realities, American novelists should concern themselves with "the more smiling aspects of life, which are the more American, and seek the universal in the individual rather than the social interests."[2]

By the time Garland wrote *Crumbling Idols*, he had accepted most of Howell's convictions expressed in *Criticism and Fiction*. However, Garland's reading and lectures during the period also indicate that he was influenced by many other critics, artists, philosophers, and scientists; and these included Emerson, Whitman, Hippolyte Taine, Frederich von Spielhagen, Darwin, Spencer, H. M. Posnett, and Eugene Véron. Garland accepted Taine's deterministic formula expressed in *History of English Literature* according to which literature or art, like natural phenomena, is the by-product of time, place, and race and which, therefore, ought to tell the truth about a nation at a particular moment in its history. In this view literature, therefore, was not only a product of the times but could be judged on the accuracy of the description rendered.

Important, too, in Garland's development of a literary theory were Herbert Spencer's evolutionary terms and ideas which he explained in detail in his *First Principles:* "Evolution is an integration of matter and concomitant dissipation of motion; during which the matter passes from an indefinite, incoherent homogeneity to a definite, coherent heterogeneity; and during which the retained motion undergoes a parallel transformation."[3] Since Spencer saw every phase of life as a progressive movement, his system was perfectly adaptable to all phases of life; and his two principal ideas that influenced American thought were a belief in progress and the need for individual liberty.[4]

In 1885, when Garland began work on a large project entitled "The Evolution of American Thought,"[5] he intended to treat American literature according to the formulas prescribed by Taine and by Spencer. About this time Garland read the recently published *Comparative Literature* in which H. M. Posnett argued that, no absolute standards can exist since literature itself depends on varying physical and social conditions. And, because literature should reflect progress, to ask modern writers to conform to past standards would be retrogressive. Since Garland was convinced of both the increased heterogeneity in modern American life and the need for a national literature, he felt that American literature should reflect contemporary American life in all its diversity and complexity. It had to deal, therefore, with the primary characteristics of the present, the common experiences of the people. Literature had to continue to evolve with life; for to write about another age, using other standards, was to be essentially untruthful.[6]

II   The Local-Color Movement

Besides Walt Whitman's works, which seemed to Garland to epitomize the foremost in contemporary literary development because of Whitman's treatment of contemporary life, the common man, and his democratic individualism, Garland felt that the local-color movement was the only existing one capable of responding to the evolutionary dictates established by Spencer and applied to literature by Posnett and Taine. To Garland, local color, which he defined simply as that which *"has such a quality of texture and background that it could not have been written in any other place or by any one else than a native,"*[7] would become the dominant literary form because it was the only one capable of depicting the diversity and complexity of American life.

In a sense, the local-color movement was a form of literary nationalism, for it not only indicated the truth of life of a particular area but minimized also the foreign influence. Garland was convinced that "each locality must produce its own literary record,"[8] and he used the leading local colorists of the day as examples of this dominant trend:

My conception of the local novel and of its great importance in American literature, especially interested the master [Howells] who listened intently while I enlarged upon my reasons for believing that the local novel would continue to grow in power and insight. At the end I said, "In my judgment the men and women of the south, the west and the east, are working (without knowing it) in accordance with a great principle, which is this: American literature, in order to be great, must be national, and in order to be national, must deal with conditions peculiar to our own land and climate. Every genuinely American writer must deal with the life he knows best and for which he cares the most. Thus Joel Chandler Harris, George W. Cable, Joseph Kirkland, Sarah Orne Jewett, and Mary Wilkins, like Bret Harte, are but varying phases of the same movement, a movement which is to give us at last a really vital and original literature!"[9]

Edward Eggleston, whom Garland later referred to as "the father of us all"[10] because of his *The Hoosier Schoolmaster* (1871) and *The*

Circuit Rider (1874), indicated the potential that rural life on the frontier offered fiction. Combined with E. W. Howe's *The Story of a Country Town* (1883) and Joseph Kirkland's *Zury: The Meanest Man in Spring County* (1887) and *The McVeys* (1888), these American, Middle West writers introduced a region not yet prominent in the local-color movement and became forerunners of Garland's middle-border fiction and especially of his *Main-Travelled Roads*.

During 1886 and 1887, while Garland was insisting on the importance of the local-color novel, he came upon Eugene Véron's *Aesthetics*, which Garland cited as a major source of ideas for *Crumbling Idols*. Like Garland, Véron, also influenced by evolutionary thought, insisted that the artist must free himself from the past and deal with the present. To enable artists to do so, Véron advocated a theory of literary impressionism; he maintained that "there are but three ways open to art: the imitation of previous forms of art; the realistic imitation of actual things; the manifestation of individual impression."[11] Of these three, the last was the essential constituent of art, for the value of impressionistic art is derived from the character and personality of the artist, corrected by observed fact: "TRUTH AND PERSONALITY: these are the alpha and omega of art formulas: *truth* as to facts, and the *personality* of the artist."[12] As Pizer suggests, Garland had no difficulty introducing Véron into his critical system, for Véron not only stressed the necessity of art to change but it required that it be accomplished through the expression of individual personality. To Garland, an individual response to observed fact was simply another way of stating the idea of local color. This procedure not only freed the artist to react personally to environment and resolved the problem of what was "real," but allowed for variation within the practice of local color.[13]

III   Crumbling Idols

Garland's literary manifesto, *Crumbling Idols*, deals with a variety of critical issues, but particular themes run throughout it. Garland emphasizes the necessity for originality and individuality in authorship, freedom from past models for modern literature, Americanism and nationalism, and a proclamation of Western literary independence. In fact, Garland clearly agreed with Howells' advice to the contemporary writer: "Do not trouble yourself about standards or ideals; but try to be faithful and natural: remember that there is no greatness, no beauty, which does not come from truth to your own knowledge of things; and keep on working, even if your work is not long remembered."[14] In the preface of *Crumbling Idols* Garland argued that

Youth should study the past, not to get away from the present, but to understand the present and to anticipate the future. I believe in the mighty pivotal present. I believe in the living, not the dead. The men and women around me interest me more than the saints and heroes of other centuries.

I do not advocate an exchange of masters, but freedom from masters. Life, Nature,—these should be our teachers. They are the masters who do not enslave.

Youth should be free from the domination of the dead; therefore I defend the individual right of the modern creative mind to create in the image of life, and not in the image of any literary master, living or dead.[15]

Garland maintained that literature should be free from foreign models; its subject matter and forms should be native. In the past, Garland observed, American literature had not depicted the American people but had relied upon foreign models. It had, in other words, been imitative, not creative. Once freed from European domination, young American writers would be able to express native themes by studying indigenous conditions in American life with which they were familiar.

He also proclaimed that future American literature would be democratic: it would concern itself with the lives of the common people. Not only did he rebel against British models, but he turned against the advocates of French naturalism. While he was influenced by the evolutionary theories of Darwin and Spencer, as were the French naturalists, Garland felt, as did Howells, that literature should not deal excessively with crime and abnormalities; it should represent characteristic types and not be preoccupied with sex, filth, and the diseased. He repeatedly complained about the morbidity of modern French literature.

While Garland basically advocated a form of literary realism, after the manner of Howells, he was concerned with the terminology of realism. In order to avoid confusion between Howells' view of realism—which aimed at a truthful representation of American life but avoided extremes by attempting to depict the commonplace—and the exponents of a "harsher realism," after the manner of Emile Zola, Garland propounded a form of literary impressionism called "veritism." For Garland, the essence of veritism was to "write of those things which you know most, and for which you care most. By doing so you will be true to yourself, true to your locality, and true to your time."[16] In a letter to Eldon C. Hill, Garland explained his use of the term:

You ask about my use of the word veritest. I began to use it in the late nineties. Not being at that time a realist in the sense in which the followers of Zola used it, I hit upon the word veritist which I may have derived from Zola. In truth I was an impressionist in that I presented life and landscape as I personally perceived them but [since] I sought a deeper significance in the use of the word which subtended verification. I sought to verify my impressions by comparing impressions separated by an interval of time—I thought to get away from the use of the word realism which implied predominant use of sexual vice and crime in the manner of Zola and certain of the German novelists. . . . I found as Whitman told me he had found in the life of the average American, a certain decorum and normality.[17]

By arguing that, at bottom, "realism," "veritism," and "Americanism" meant "practically the same thing,"[18] and by distinguishing between his form of realism and that practiced by the followers of Zola, Garland resolved the problem of defending traditional morality within the limits imposed by accurate observation and realistic detail. Like James, Howells, and the early Twain, Garland's realism was infused with a strain of ethical idealism which implied moral responsibility and an abiding faith in man's moral nature. Garland's Veritism differs from Howellsian realism because of his emphasis on impressionism, an insistence on the centrality of the artist's individual vision. Though Garland's depiction of farm life in *Main-Travelled Roads* is harsher than Howells' suggestion that literature should deal with the "more smiling aspects of life," Garland's ethical idealism and his romantic individualism precluded his accepting the view of life and the treatment of material practiced by Zola's followers. Garland summarized his attitude in the following terms:

The realist or veritist is really an optimist, a dreamer. He sees life in terms of what it might be, as well as in terms of what it is; but he writes of what is, and, at his best, suggests what is to be by contrast. He aims to be perfectly truthful in his delineation of his relation to life, but there is a tone, a color which comes unconsciously into his utterance, like a sobbing stir of the muted violins beneath the frank, clear song of the clarionet; and this tone is one of sorrow that the good time moves so slowly in its approach.[19]

Despite its tone which appeared radical to many literary critics of the time, *Crumbling Idols* reveals Garland's acceptance of the prevailing literary mores of the 1890s and his firm belief in traditional moral values. And it provides an insight into Garland's apparent "decline from realism," which, given his own definition, was not so sudden or so inconsistent as it appears on the surface. Even Garland's literature of social protest in the 1890s indicates that he was, above all, an idealistic realist.

CHAPTER 3

Early Middle Border Fiction

I Crude Beginnings

WHILE Garland made several unsuccessful attempts at writing fiction during his stay in Boston before 1887, he was primarily involved in functioning as a teacher, critic, and lecturer. He was attempting to write some fiction as early as 1885; but his notebook of this year contains several unfinished stories which he never tried to complete or publish later. Garland did, however, manage to publish his first story in the magazine *Every Other Saturday* in March, 1885.[1] The story, as Garland later recalled, was influenced by Hawthorne and made incidental use of Midwestern material.[2] In "Ten Years Dead" the narrator meets a man named Gregory, the son of a Western farmer, in a Chicago library. Gregory, who had previously suffered an attack of brain fever, had remained in a coma for ten years and on awakening had retained no recollection of what had happened during the period of his illness—despite an attempt to recall the lost period of his life. While Garland placed the action of the story in the West, he had not yet learned to develop themes and characters from Western life.

However, when Garland revisited Dakota in 1887 to gather fictional material, he was morally outraged at what he encountered. He was still idealistic enough to be capable of moral indignation against economic injustices which brought about tragedy and despair for the farmer. In his next two stories, "A Common Case" and "John Boyle's Conclusion," Garland depicted the barrenness and futility of Western farm life. "A Common Case" (which he later retitled "Before the Low Green Door," including it *Wayside Courtships* in 1897, but omitting the first section) was written in the spring of 1888, and was his first story to be published after "Ten Years Dead."

This second published story deals with Matilda Bent, a defeated farm wife. Through Garland's surrogate spokesman, Rance Knapp, the author discusses the dying mother who "has lived in that miserable little hovel for a quarter of a century. She has heard nothing, seen nothing of the grandeur and glory of this great age we boast about, . . . the American farmer living in semi-solitude, his wife a slave, both denied the things that make life worth living. Fifty per cent of these farms mortaged, in spite of the labors of every member of the family and the most frugal living."[3]

In the second half of the story Garland painfully depicts how Matilda dies: resentful of her husband, the farm, and the world, she desires only peace and rest. Also since Garland had been moving rapidly to becoming a propaganist for the single tax, the story implicitly discusses the tragedy of farm life which Garland felt was the direct result of unfair economic and social conditions. Even at this early stage in his career Garland was already becoming the literary spokesman for the discontented farmers of the middle-border.

"John Boyle's Conclusion," written in 1888, after Garland had revisited the West, is similar in tone, theme, and framework to "A Common Case"[4]; but this later story was also one of the bitterest stories Garland was ever to write. The story deals with the effects of farm life on the Boyles, John and Sairy, an elderly farm couple, and on Porter and Ida Alling, a young couple. By contrasting two reactions to a devastating hail storm, Garland effectively dramatizes the effect of the continuous defeats on the Boyles. The Boyles have previously lost several farms because of war and because of financial problems created by a praire fire and by cinch bugs. In July, the Boyles are again on the verge of losing their farm because of a drought. The Boyles' hopes are momentarily raised when they think a coming storm will bring the necessary rain. However, a devastating hail storm occurs that not only ruins the crops for the last time but breaks John Boyle's spirit.

In the second part of the story, the point of view shifts away from the Boyles to Porter and Ida Alling, a young couple, who are also ruined by the storm. But, because they are still young, they are able to absorb the defeat and to decide to leave farm life. They function not so much to suggest that escape is possible (although Garland himself escaped the hardships of farm life early in his own life), but to comment on the social, economic, and natural conditions that bring about tragedy:

What can such people as the Boyles be living for? Nothing but poverty, suffering, and certain death for a few years laters. . . . Do you know I'm getting skeptical concerning this "great and glorious" of ours. A land that produces and maintains so many citizens like Boyle and myself ain't just the kind I'd care to support forever. It may be high honor to live and work as we do, but it don't appear that way to us. Rising at dawn the year round and working till dark every day in order to rear a family in honest way, or picking coal in a seam at forty cents a ton may be the ideal condition of things, but it does not appeal to me so.[5]

After the storm, the Allings go to the Boyle farm only to find that the farm is ruined, that Sairy Boyle has gone mad, and that John has committed suicide by drowning.

While the dialogue is somewhat crude and while Garland gets melodramtic in some scenes and propagandizes too much in others, the story powerfully evokes a sympathetic response to the plight of the Boyles. Moreover, Garland's treatment of nature contributes to his themes. In a way similar to Stephen Crane in "The Open Boat," it appears to John Boyle as if "All the stupendous forces of nature, so blind and so unalterable, unite to torture or to crush out such an infinitesimal mote as this man. Just as one might imagine a tempest, a thunderbolt, and a glacier uniting to destroy a sand fly lean with hunger. In fact, however, the man and the fly chance—if we may use the word chance—to be in the confidence of world wide forces as they march on their unchangeable courses, and there results the apparently vindicative assault of unseeing and insentient powers."[6] Garland's nature is neither malevolent nor benevolent; it is merely indifferent. More often, however, Garland is much more ambivalent about his view of nature.

"John Boyle's Conclusion" and "A Common Case" are important in Garland's development because the theme, the tone, and the subject foreshadow the direction of his fiction for the next several years. Also, by this time, Garland had become committed to the local-color story and the "new realism"; and his locale was to be the middle-border.

II Main-Travelled Roads

The years from 1888 to 1890 were prolific ones for Garland; in addition to writing plays and novelettes, most of his stories during the period were collected in *Main-Travelled Roads* (1891) and *Prairie Folks* (1893). Nonetheless, Garland was having difficulty getting his material published; and he was therefore happy, as has been noted earlier, to become acquainted at this time with B. O. Flower, the radical editor of the *Arena*. Early in 1891 Flower suggested that Garland collect some of his stories in a volume to be published by the Arena Publishing Company, a subsidiary of the *Arena*. Also, in 1891, on a commission from the *Arena*, Garland toured the West and completed his populist novel, *A Spoil of Office*. In June, 1891, *Main-Travelled Roads* appeared with the subtitle "Six Mississippi Valley Stories." One of these six, "The Return of the Private," had first appeared in the *Arena;* and "Under the Lion's Paw," "Among the Corn Rows," and "Mrs. Ripley's Trip" had already been published in *Harper's Weekly*. "A Branch Road" and "Up the Coule" saw first publication in the 1891 edition. Later, in an 1899 edition, Garland added three new stories: "The Creamery Man," "A Day's Pleasure," and "Uncle Ethan Ripley"; in the 1922 edition, "God's Ravens" and "A 'Good Fellow's' Wife" were incorporated. And finally in 1930 Garland added "Martha's Fireplace."

While several of the stories in the volume are flawed, the book as a whole is a powerful and evocative treatment of Western farm life. Its poignant portrayal of man's struggles against the forces of nature and social injustices led Howells to observe that,

If any one is still at a loss to account for that uprising of farmers in the West which is the translation of the Peasant's War into modern and republican terms, let him read *Main-Travelled Roads*, and he will begin to understand, unless, indeed, Mr. Garland is painting the exceptional rather than the average. The stories are full of those gaunt, grim, sordid, pathetic, ferocious figures, whom our satirists find so easy to caricature as Hayseeds, and whose blind groping for fairer conditions is so grotesque to the newspapers and so menacing to the politicians. They feel that something is wrong, and they know that the wrong is not theirs. The type caught in Mr. Garland's book is not pretty; it is ugly and often ridiculous; but it is heart-breaking in its rude despair.[7]

Garland uses the metaphor of the Western road as the symbolic structural center for *Main-Travelled Roads*, and he also employs in the first edition an epigraph before each story to achieve unity. A prefatory statement introducing the volume sets the dominant tone and Contains a hint of what is to follow:

The main-travelled road in the West (as everywhere) is hot and dusty in summer, and desolate and drear with mud in fall and spring, and in winter the winds sweep the snow across it; but it does sometimes cross a rich meadow where the songs of the larks and bobolinks and blackbirds are tangled. Follow it far enough, it may lead past a bend in the river where the water laughs eternally over its shallows.

Mainly it is long and wearyful and has a dull little town at one end, and a home of toil at the other. Like the main-travelled road of life, it is traversed by many classes of people, but the poor and the weary predominate.[8]

Throughout this volume Garland emphasizes that, while farm life was sometimes tragic and generally desolate and dreary, it also contained exhilarating moments.

Unlike many local-color stories of the time that sentimentally expressed the charm of quaint country villages and that characterized American rural life as a pastoral idyll, the stories in *Main-Travelled Roads* express outrage at the social injustices suffered by the farmer. Perhaps because, from the time of the nation's first settlement, America had been viewed as a land of boundless opportunity for which the West symbolized an Edenic paradise, Garland felt compelled to inform Eastern readers about the true realities of farm life. Garland's tendency to destroy this myth is clearly present in all of the stories as they depict the ugliness, monotony, and hopelessness of the average American farmer. But it is also possible to overemphasize Garland's disillusionment; for, despite the pervasive deterministic forces present, a persistent strain of romantic optimism is evident.

Moreover, Garland reflects an ethical idealism which sets him at odds with the naturalists who believed that, since man was determined by forces over which he had no control, he necessarily had less moral responsibility. Throughout, Garland persistently stresses the strength of the individual will. While it is true that Garland's realistic portrayal of hardship did much to shatter any romanticism about the American pastoral idyll, and that the submission of many of his characters to the inevitable demands of the world suggest the futility of farm life, his characters also continue to strive because of their will. Since many of the stories have a hopeful ending, they also indicate and justify Garland's compassionate view of human nature and his love for the land. As Robert Mane observes, love remains possible; and, if it does not lighten the burden, it is at least a compensation which makes life tolerable. And, thanks to children, happiness always remains possible, and solitude is banished. This moral of the lack of isolation and companionship contradicts the diffused pessimism of the stories. Such an ambiguity, far from an impediment, gives to Garland's work and to his characters both value and vitality.[9]

This ambivalence of isolation and companionship, and optimism and pessimism, is illustrated in "The Return of the Private," a moving story of post - Civil War disillusionment. Private Smith's return is filled with high expectations, and his first views of his land justify those expectations. But, despite the beauty of the landscape, his harmony with nature, and the hospitality of the neighbors, the return of the exhausted, aged veteran is not pleasant because he finds his farm in shambles. But the story does not end on this despondent note, for a gradual transformation of Smith into a Whitmanesque archtypic hero occurs: "His war with the South was over, and his fight, his daily running fight, with nature and against the injustice of his fellow-men was begun again. In the dusk of that far-off valley his figure looms vast, his personal peculiarities fade away, he rises into a magnificant type."[10] But, more importantly, his reunion with his wife banishes their loneliness and compensates for the renewed drudgery which they both must now face.

In "A Branch Road" this ambivalence is most clearly expressed. In this story, Will Hannan, who has left the farm to make his way in life, returns seven years later only to discover the pitiable condition of his former sweetheart, who has since married and reared a family on the farm. In the first half of the story, the rustic idyll seems to be confirmed by an ecstasy for nature that is as lyrical and poetic as anything in Whitman; and the observer is Will Hannan, a romantic young man, who seems uncommonly sensitive to the divine beauty in nature. As the dawn unfolds, the reader is treated to scene after scene that depicts nature as both beautiful and bountiful; and the farmer depicts a mystical relationship with nature in the ritual of the harvest.

When Will returns to this land after his long absence, he finds on the surface the same idyllic beauty in the rural landscape. Standing on a bridge amid a display of nature, he peers into a brook and contemplates the apparent sameness. But there is trouble in paradise: A water snake appears and sends the happily swimming minnows scurrying under the bridge. His reverie broken, Will decides that there is "something prophetic" in the incident. Then, much like Garland himself who returned to the West after several years in Boston and found his mother in a desolate state, Will finds his former sweetheart married to an insensitive brute. Living in squalor, her beauty gone, her health failing, she has been beaten by her life of toil.

This return-of-the-native theme, a recurring one in Garland's works, is also an American version (or inversion) of the prodigal son's return. The American boy does not go forth and squander his inheritance; he goes away, earns his money, and returns home. When he returns he is either driving a herd of white-faced, fatted calves before him or carrying their current market value in greenbacks. Although Will leaves his cattle in Arizona, he does bring home money and guilt. Remorse is added to guilt when he discovers that his needless desertion and social injustices have ruined Agnes' life. Unlike his biblical prototype, Will brings prosperity, his expectations are high, and his first glimpse of the land reinforces these expectations; but he finds his loved one in ruin. Only at this point does he realize that his own life has been a waste.

Again, however, the story does not end on a despondent note. Will persuades Agnes to flee with him into a completely new life despite the fact that she is still married to Grant, and the story closes with the sun shining "on the dazzling, rustling wheat, the fathomless sky blue, as a sea, bent about them."[11] Howells judged the end to be morally wrong; but Garland, as he was later to do in *A Little Norsk*, intended to oppose the sacred right of individuals to conventional morals.

A spirit of guilt permeates several stories in the volume, a theme that unquestionably resulted from Garland's personal guilt over the plight of his family, and especially of his mother.[12] In "Up the Coule," the most powerful and in a sense the most autobiographical story in the volume, Garland again dramatizes his own sense of guilt toward his family and his subsequent fear that he would be unable to compensate for his desertion by depicting the return of Howard McLane, a successful actor, to Wisconsin from the East to visit his mother and brother, Grant. In the story, Garland uses several contrasts to present his theme, but he also creates a vivid sense of the emptiness and hopelessness of life on the farm. Two of these contrasts are most important: the beauty of the countryside contrasts with the paucity of beauty in the lives of the farmers, and the contrast between the life-styles of Howard and Grant. But the most striking tension is contained in the conflict between success and failure.

When Howard returns home he is overcome by the beauty of the mountains and valleys and by the pastoral, peaceful scene of his boyhood. In the beginning, we do not see Grant; the point of view is entirely Howard's. He is aware of "dazzling sunlight flamed along the luscious velvety grass, and shot amid the rounded, distant purple peaks, and streamed in bars of gold and crimson across the blue mist of the narrower upper Coules."[13] As he gazed upon the land with dreaming eyes, it had "a certain mysterious glamour to him; the lakes were cooler and brighter to his eye, the greens fresher, and the grain more golden than to any one else, for he was coming back to it all after an absence of ten years. It was, besides, *his* West. He still took pride in being a Western man."[14] The men who lounge at the railway station, though poor and dirty, have a simple innocence about them. Howard feels pleasure in being able to ride silently beside William McTurg, who knew that "silence was the only speech amid such splendors."[15] Ironically, McTurg is not silent because he is in awe of nature "of whose beauty he never spoke"; he is so weighted down with the burdens of existence that he is unaware of nature's splendor.

But Howard is immediately forced to see the "poor and dull and sleepy and squalid" town whose buildings are "drab-colored, miserable, rotting."[16] When Howard confronts his brother Grant and his family he finds them living in poverty on a small, unproductive farm; for the family property has been sold to pay a mortgage. Grant's colorless, muddy farm contrasts with the sparkling white cuffs and collar of Howard's shirt. Grant makes it plain that he blames Howard for the loss of the farm; for he is convinced that, had Howard shared his wealth, he could have saved the farm and spared his mother much misery. And Howard's gifts of fine silk from Paris, a parasol for Grant's wife, and a copy, ironically, of General Grant's autobiography for Grant additionally enrage his brother. But societal pressures and injustices have led inevitably to Grant's somber view of life: he feels hopelessly trapped. "A man like me is helpless," he remarks. "Just like a fly in a pan of molasses. There ain't any escape for him. The more he tears around the more liable he is to rip his legs off."[17]

Although Howard clearly feels superior to his brother and farm life, he eventually is overcome by his guilt and admits his selfishness and neglect and offers to make amends for his desertion by buying back the old farm; but the story ends as Grant, all hope gone and full of despair, refuses Howard's assistance. As Pizer observes, Garland's joining of superiority and selfishness has a twofold meaning for his work and career: it represents the particular configuration which he gave to his powerful sense of guilt in his early work. But it also anticipates his gradual estrangement from the area in which Garland himself felt socially and aesthetically superior.[18] But Garland also implies here, as later, that Grant's destruction is not primarily the result of Howard's neglect; it was really caused by the overpowering evils of contemporary farm conditions. In other words, Grant's life was ultimately determined by economic factors over which he had no control.

While "Up the Coule" suggests inequities in the economic system, "Under the Lion's Paw," the best-known story in the collection, is the only story which explicitly makes use of the single-tax doctrine. Henry George had argued that land speculation and the absentee land owner would be impossible if all land in a specific area were taxed as if it were in full use by the owner; and, since no one could afford to own unused land if such a tax system were adopted, only the user would be the possessor of the land. Written as an illustration of Henry George's thesis of the harmful social effect of the unearned increment, Garland habitually used the text when he was lecturing and campaigning for Populist candidates. The Haskins family, forced to settle in Kansas because of the high price of land in the East, is plagued by grasshoppers and forced to move again. Aided by a hospitable family, they rent a farm in Iowa from Jim Butler, a villainous land speculator. After three years of hard labor, Haskins is ready to buy, but Butler doubles the price because of the improvements Haskins himself made upon the land. The banker, who has done nothing, will get the profits; and, because of his rage at the injustice of the situation, Haskins determines to murder Butler. However, Haskins refrains from carrying out his purpose when he sees his own child; and, though crushed under the economic system, he resolves to renew his struggle for her sake.

Generally, Garland's treatment of farm life is anti-idyllic; and, because of the harsh demands of that life, his treatment of the possibilities of romantic love is no less so. The emotional center of many of the stories is the demoralizing condition of the farmer's wife. Cut off from human community, she is destined to a depressing, lonely life and has no hope of fulfillment. Some, like Agnes in "A Branch Road" or Nellie Sanford in "A Good Fellow's Wife," are fortunate enough to escape before they are utterly ruined. Others, like Delia Markham in "A Day's Pleasure" or Grandma Ripley in "Mrs. Ripley's Trip," are afforded temporary release from their montonous routine. But the point is always the same: the loneliness and hardships for which a prairie wife is destined serve as an ironic comment on the beauty of the landscape and finally defeat our expectations of romantic love.

This tension is perhaps best illustrated in "Among the Corn

Rows." The story presents a courtship and an elopement which is born out of economic considerations that become coupled to vague, subconscious unrealized urges. In the first section, we are given an account of Rob's life on the prairie and his practical reasons for wanting a wife. In the second section, Rob's courtship of Julia is described, amid the beauty of the landscape and her romantic expectations. But Garland treats his theme with a certain ambiguity. The explicit advocacy of a belief in man as a rational creature is set against a prose style which seems to undercut that belief. The result is a curious tension not only between desire and reality, but between the two views of the nature of man in which the force of the sensual prose style, with the implications of subconscious urges which it carries, threatens to engulf the strength of the individual will of Rob and Julia.

In part 2, imagery, simile, and metaphor combine in the lyrical prose style to create a mood and atmosphere so thoroughly sensual that it nearly engulfs both Rob and Julia. The description of nature corresponds to the emotions of the moment: "He stopped at length, and turning, watched the girl moving along in the deeps of the corn. Hardly a leaf was stirring; the untempered sunlight fell in a burning flood upon the field; the grasshoppers rose, snapped, buzzed, and fell; the locust uttered its dry, heat-intensifying cry. The man lifted his head."[19] But ultimately his emotion is suppressed and the beauty of the landscape cannot conceal the loneliness for which Julia is destined:

> He saw her go to the house, and then he turned and walked slowly up the dusty road. Out of the May-weed the grasshoppers sprang, buzzing and snapping their dull red wings. Butterflies, yellow and white, fluttered around moist places in the ditch, and slender striped water-snakes glided across the stagnant pools at the sound of footsteps.
>
> But the mind of the man was far away on his claim, building a new house, with a woman's advice and presence.[20]

The 1891 edition of *Main-Travelled Roads* appropriately closes with a tender, moving story about the relationship of an old couple who are settled into the burdens and hardships of daily life and who have little to which to look forward. Frustrated with her life, Mrs. Ripley desires to make a last trip to the East where she was born, but she feels guilty about leaving her husband, even for a short time. However, she finally accomplishes her dream, and then returns to the farm to resume her misery. "Her trip was a fact now;

no chance could rob her of it. She had looked forward twenty-three years toward it, and now she could look back at it accomplished. She took up her burden again, never more thinking to lay it down."[21]

Garland's later additions to *Main-Travelled Roads*, though the stories deal with the same subject matter and focus particularly on the farm wife, disturb the tight unity of the first edition. These later stories tend to be milder, to lack the possibility of tragedy and the sense of outrage at farm conditions that characterize the original text. Though the stories contain some of Garland's best writing and create some memorable characters, with the exception of the moving "A Day's Pleasure" the subtle tensions and stark contrasts which give the original text its vitality are lacking. In "A Day's Pleasure" Markham takes his wife and child from the farm to the city for a day. Mrs. Markham's misery is temporarily relieved by a sympathetic acquaintence. However, since the relief is only temporary, the return to the grim conditions of the farm seems even more depressing since she has been given a taste of human companionship.

Frequently the stories, like much of Garland's later fiction, are more anecdotal expressions and lack the deeper emotions of the people.

But, taken as a whole, and particularly considering the original text, *Main-Travelled Roads* is Garland's best book. It is not only a significant social and historical document, but, despite its flaws, illustrates Garland's capacity to artistically transform personal feelings, attitudes, and experiences into compelling themes for his fiction.

III   Prairie Folks

Although *Prairie Folks* (1893) appeared two years later than *Main-Travelled Roads*, its stories were written about the same time. In fact, Garland, himself, thought of it as a "companion volume" to the earlier collection. The 1893 edition of *Prairie Folks* initially contained nine stories, but later, as in *Main-Travelled Roads*, Garland made additions. While *Prairie Folks* is never given the prominence of *Main-Travelled Roads*, the two volumes are closely related, as Garland intended. In both volumes, the presiding subject matter is farm life; many of the same characters appear in both volumes; and Garland precedes each story with a poem which sets the tone for the story which follows.

Robert Mane, however, indicates two important differences between *Prairie Folks* and *Main-Travelled Roads*. In *Prairie Folks*, there is an insistence on the life of the community; in *Main-Travelled Roads*, the emphasis is on the individual. And the movement in *Prairie Folks* is more accentuated toward the romantic.[22] With the exception of "Sim Burn's Wife," the stories are similar in tone to the later additions to *Main-Travelled Roads* which Garland made after the 1891 volume and generally to his fiction after 1895. Several stories in the volume which belong to Garland's "lighter" or "milder" fiction reflect his attraction to Richard Watson Gilder rather than to B. O. Flower.

"A Spring Romance" specifically belongs to these milder stories which do not portray the hardships and toil of farm life. Here, Lyman Gilman, working for William Bacon, decides to marry Bacon's daughter, Marietta. Bacon, however, whose wife and only son are dead, is enraged, feeling that he has a claim on Marietta. Although Lyman is told to leave the farm, he returns at night and convinces Marietta to elope with him. They leave together, but they return after they are married to live with Bacon. He finally accepts the marriage.

Garland uses the escape-return motif here as he did frequently in *Main-Travelled Roads* and also suggests the difficulty of freedom for women; but, unlike his other stories, he does not hint at the drudgery of farm life awaiting the couple (especially Marietta) when they resume their place on the farm. Rather, the story focuses on a romantic interlude in the spring which, when isolated from the total picture of farm life, suggests the possibilities of romantic love. Since there is no complication of nature and since youth and love triumph, these circumstances contrast with Garland's more frequent treatment of the irrelevance of romantic love and the beauty of nature.

Both "The Test of Elder Pill" and "A Day of Grace" give a flavor of the times, especially the flavor of medieval religion. The philosophy of both episodes is a plea for simple humanitarianism; if heaven exists, people must know how to find it on this earth. Donald Pizer suggests that "The Test of Elder Pill" dramatizes a Spencerian distrust of the "barbarism" of evangelism and calls for an earnest "morality" to replace "antiquated terrorism" as Elder (Andrew) Pill comes to town to preach.[23] Through an ambitious evangelism, he throws terror into the hearts of his listeners. However, in the middle of one of his sermons William Bacon interrupts him; cynic Radbourne follows him; and Pill is defeated. After seeking advice from Radbourne, Pill meditates on his "old morality" and realizes that, although he has no religion left, he still has morality. He leaves, eventually returns to preaching, but the changed man has replaced terrorism with humanitarianism.

Drawing upon a similar theme, "A Day of Grace" deals with the antiquated terrorism of the revival meeting and with the emotional excesses of rural religion. Although Ben Griswold saves Grace Cole from "falling" under the influence of the preacher at the meeting, Ben changes as a result of his experience at the meeting and his growing closeness to "Grace."

The most powerful story in the volume is "Sim Burn's Wife." There is little in this story, which fully treats the despair of the farm wife, that lightens its pessimism. Lucretia Burns is initially described in a realistic, unromantic way: "It was a pitfully warm, almost tragic face—long, thin, sallow, hollow-eyed. The mouth had long since lost the power to shape itself into a kiss, and had a droop at the corners which seemed to announce a breaking-down at any moment into a despairing wail. The collarless neck and sharp shoulders showed painfully. And even Sim Burns had long since ceased to kiss his wife or even to speak kindly to her. There was no longer any sanctity to life or love."[24] The story dramatizes the sympathetic feeling Garland had for a farm wife. For Lucretia, there is no escape from her monotonous, unromantic life. She contemplates suicide, but finally resolves to go on. Like several stories in *Main-Travelled Roads*, the tone tends toward despair, but the characters have an abiding endurance and cannot be defeated. Again Garland places the blame on economic conditions which produce the misery. Through Radbourne, the young radical, Garland explicitly voices his views on the economic system, specifically insisting that the downfall of the farmer can be directly attributed to his economic condition.

The story, although powerful, reveals a basic incapacity Garland had in his future fiction: he cannot control his penchant for intruding into the narrative to propagandize about socioeconomic conditions of the time. His point is made dramatically enough without his intervention.

In a lighter vein, in "Some Village Cronies," Garland deals with the baiting of Colonel Peavy about his bald head by Squire Gordon during a checker game at the town grocery one winter evening. A humorous story, Garland presents in it well-drawn local types and focuses on the local, colorful scene. This story was not a product of Garland's reaction against conditions in the West but of his nostalgic memories of his life as a boy.

Like "Some Village Cronies," "Daddy Deering" also belongs to Garland's "milder fiction." It is a simple, uncomplicated tale of a vibrant, fun-loving man who simply grows old and dies. There is not much dramatic tension in the story, except at the end when, for a brief moment, we suspect that Daddy Deering has committed suicide. But we find that Daddy, knowing he was going to die, went out into the snow to "defiantly meet his death." The story does not depict the tragedy and toil of farm life. Daddy is vibrant as long as he can work. It is only when he cannot function, when old age comes and the past becomes a nostalgic memory, that the character is pitiable. But he never succumbs to despair.

"Drifting Crane" illustrates Garland's early interest in the Indian problem and announces a long series of stories to come. Here, Chief Drifting Crane tries to convince Henry Wilson, a solitary pioneer, to leave his ranch which borders an Indian reservation. But Wilson refuses and tries to explain to Drifting Crane that the Indian's fate is doomed, that the white settlers will eventually come. Garland briefly indicates the injustices of the whites in their treatment of the Indian and his land. At the same time, he attempts to evoke the tragedy of a dying race.

Prairie Folks, like *Main-Travelled Roads*, dealt with material which Garland knew well. The pleasant scenes Garland depicts were as much a part of his personal experiences as a result of growing up in the West as were the pitiable pictures found in *Main-Travelled Roads*. But though the stories in *Prairie Folks* depict a wide range of Western material, though the picturesque renderings of the local scenes are memorable, and though the volume has an attractive lyrical quality that is reinforced by the quoted poems which run throughout, the volume ultimately suffers from the distinct lack of sufficient plot and character development. It fails to touch the "deeper life" of a people which *Main-Travelled Roads* accomplishes so well. It fails mainly because here Garland withheld the possibility of tragedy that was always threatening in *Main-Travelled Roads*. The lighter aspects of life depicted in *Prairie Folks* were unquestionably found a part of the farmers' experiences, but their lives contained much more. And such failure to capture their total lives, while frequently pleasant, ultimately harms the volume. This failure anticipates Garland's later failures in his longer fiction after 1895.

CHAPTER 4

Economic Fiction
and the Populist Revolt

I   Political and Economic Background

DURING the last quarter of the nineteenth century many forces contributed to the growth of widespread and bitter discontentment among farmers in the West and elsewhere. In 1887 a farm journal in North Carolina echoed the general feeling of farmers throughout the United States:

There is something radically wrong in our industrial system. There is a screw loose. The wheels have dropped out of balance. The railroads have never been so prosperous, and yet agriculture languishes. The banks have never done a better or more profitable business, and yet agriculture languishes. Manufacturing enterprises never made more money or were in a more flourishing condition, and yet agriculture languishes. Towns and cities flourish and "boom," and yet agriculture languishes. Salaries and fees were never so temptingly high and desirable, and yet agriculture languishes.[1]

Common grievances acted powerfully to draw together the farmers of the agricultural South and of the agricultural West. It was commonly felt that sinister forces restrained agriculture while industry continued to rise in prosperity. The farmer never doubted that his general loss of prosperity resulted from the low prices he received from his products. The period from 1870 to 1897 was one of steadily declining prices, and a deflationary fiscal policy during this period caused the value of the dollar to appreciate nearly three hundred percent and to make the payment of mortgages even more difficult.

While many politicians and others argued that overproduction was the root of the evil, believing that this condition was due to the rapid expansion of the agricultural frontier in the United States, the

51

farmers and their defenders refused to accept this theory. The Northern farm owner was always on the verge of losing his property to the mortgage holder and the Southern cotton grower could never get out of debt; but the Western farmers had the greater grievance against the railroads, by means of which all Western crops were sent to market. But the South, no less than the West, knew how railroad companies watered their stock, granted rebates, charged high rates due to overcapitalization, evaded taxation, bought favors with free passes, and generally discriminated among shippers and shipping points. Both the South and West recorded intense protests against the tolls paid to trusts and middlemen, the high taxes for farm land, and the steadily appreciating value of the dollar.

In the West after the crises of 1887, which Garland viewed firsthand on his trip to the West, interest rates rose even higher. In Kansas, for example, from 1889 to 1893, over eleven thousand farm mortgages were foreclosed, and in some counties as much as ninety percent of the farm lands were taken over by the loan companies. The prospect of a new alliance between the dominantly agricultural sections of the country against the creditor East seemed inevitable.

The farmers' rebellion went through several phases and involved a series of separate organizations. First was the Granger movement, which emerged in the decade following the Civil War and was primarily directed against railroad abuses. Its followers argued the right of states to regulate the railroads, if necessary to the point of fixing maximum rates; but, because of business failures, the movement began to decline in popularity about 1876. Paralleling but outlasting the Grangers were the Greenbackers and Free Silverites, both determined to remedy the farmers' plight by some degree of money inflation. Farmers tended to listen to soft money arguments and to the prospect of expanded currency if it could help raise their prices. In the 1800s the Farmers' Alliances, one in the Northwest and one in the South, which had been inspired originally with ambitious programs of cooperative buying and selling, replaced the Grangers. Eventually determined to seek political as well as economic remedies, the Alliance elected several candidates on the Democratic ticket to congress in the election of 1890. Then, as an outgrowth of the Alliances and a final culmination of the agrarian crusade, came the Populist (or People's) Party, which made a place in its platform for all previously proposed reforms and added several more of its own.

In addition to the specific concerns of the farmers advocating reforms during the period, one cannot overlook the impact and influence of Edward Bellamy's *Looking Backward* (1888) on the formation and eventual political platform of the Populist Party. The publication of *Looking Backward* produced the spontaneous formation of numerous Nationalist or Bellamy clubs throughout the United States and Europe. As Sylvia Bowman points out, the Nationalist movement, in which Bellamy was to play an important part, followed two stages in its development. During the first stage, from 1888 to 1891, the clubs devoted themselves primarily to moral crusades, advocating reform measures and ideas put forth in *Looking Backward*. During the second stage, from 1891 to 1896, the Nationalists entered the field of political action, first with their own local party ticket, and then as important supporters of the Populists. Specifically and politically, Bellamy advocated a program calling for the reform of the civil service and government ownership of coal mines, express service, telephone and telegraph companies, and railroads.[2]

In April, 1891, the Nationalists received an invitation to join the People's Party and to send their representatives to the convention for formation of the party, which was to be held in Cincinnati on May 19, 1891. It was clear that the platform adopted by the People's Party was the result of the influence of *Looking Backward* and the Nationalist movement. It was also clear that Nationalism had a wide influence upon specific groups—the Farmers' Alliance, the Grangers, The Knights of Labor, woman's suffrage, and several labor unions—which were represented in the People's Party. Ignatius Donnelly, national lecturer for the Grangers and chairman of the Cincinnati platform who wrote most of the platform which was adopted by the Omaha convention in July, 1892, cited Bellamy's direct influence. William Dean Howells also felt that Bellamy "virtually founded the Populist Party."[3]

When the Populist Party met in Omaha in July, 1892, they nominated a presidential candidate, General James B. Weaver of Iowa. However, though he was never prone to be too clear about his stand relative to the impact of Bellamy, Garland certainly knew in detail what the party stood for and his books directly and indirectly contain socioeconomic ideas and criticisms resulting from his participation in the Populist movement. Garland, a single-tax enthusiast, did not participate in the Populist revolt after the election of 1892. Donald Pizer suggests that the cause of his withdrawal seems to have been that the Populist Party did not become a single-tax party, but moved in another direction. Single-tax Populists had made some progress in embodying single-tax doctrine in the Populist program. However, after 1892, and particularly after the panic and depression of 1893, the free-silver question emerged as the dominant concern of the Populist leaders.[4] While many described the free-silver issue as a "fake," calling it the "cowbird of the reform movement," its appeal continued until the defeat of William Jennings Bryan and the Populist-Democratic Party in the election of 1896. After this date, Populism ceased to be a national power; and the Democratic Party directed its efforts toward other issues.

II   Participation in the Populist Revolt

Besides several of his short stories, Garland's economic fiction primarily consists of three novels published in 1892: *Jason Edwards, A Member of the Third House*, and *A Spoil of Office*. *A Little Norsk*, which was also published in 1892, does not really shed much light on his economic attitudes. Of these four, only the last half of *A Spoil of Office* was an original work. *Jason Edwards* and *A Member of the Third House* were originally dramas which Garland transformed into novels; *A Little Norsk* was completed in 1888; and the first half of *A Spoil of Office* was written sometime during 1888 - 1889.

Most of Garland's activities and fiction of 1891 - 1892 resulted from his participation in the Populist revolt.[5] During this time, Garland joined the Anti-poverty Society and traveled extensively speaking in favor of farmers' grievances. During November, 1891, he actively campaigned in Iowa for the Farmers' Alliance; and in November, 1892, he campaigned in Iowa for the People's Party. As he later recalled when speaking of his *Jason Edwards*, the novel was of value "only as an indication of the bitter and accusing mood of that day, a time of parlor-socialists, single-taxes, militant populists, and Tolstoyan encyclicals against greed, lust, and caste."[6]

While Garland was always sympathetic to the farmer's revolt, he was primarily interested in the issue of the single tax which he felt was the farmer's most effective hope for reform. He had read, as we have seen, Henry George's *Progress and Poverty* and agreed with George that the most pervasive of social evils was monopoly of land. As George argued, to destroy poverty it is necessary to destroy monopoly in land, which could only be done by confiscatory economic rent. To confiscate rent, it is necessary only to levy a single-tax upon the land sufficient to take back to society all income which flows from the land itself, as distinguised from the user's own labor or improvements. Once this is accomplished land speculation and exploitation would cease. Garland felt, with George, that "the effect of the tax on land values is precisely like that of opening new land to settlement. It brings out the speculator's hands into the settler's hands. It passes out of the hands of the monopolist into the hands of the contractor and builder."[7] However, as Walter Taylor points out, Garland rejects all tendencies toward collectivism. The difficulties of the farmers are not due, as the socialists claim, to free competition, but to the lack of it. The interference of government in business ought to be diminished rather than increased. The primary causes of human suffering lie not in nature, but in the unjust laws of man.[8]

Garland did not participate, however, in the Populist revolt after the 1892 election, because it had become clear that the Populists did not embrace the single-tax but had begun moving in other directions, particularly in the area of free silver which Garland believed ignored the issue. Although he continued his single-tax activity after 1892, it was clear that he had become disillusioned in his expectation of seeing farmers' grievances in land reform embodied in a national political party. As Donald Pizer indicates, "the effect of this dampening was neither immediate nor superficial. Rather, it marked the beginning of the decline of his intense emotional response to the idea of reform. Although Garland was to consider himself a reformer for many years, never again did his reform fervor reach the evangelical pitch it had attained during the period from 1887 to 1892. And never again did it reach a level at which he was forced to identify the artist so completely with the reformer."[9]

III   Jason Edwards

In January, 1892, *Jason Edwards: An Average Man* was published. Originally the work had been published as a play *Under the Wheel* in the July, 1890, issue of the *Arena*. The plot, characters, and dialogue are identical in both works; the major difference is that Garland necessarily provides a more extensive background in the novel. Garland took the original title of the play from Bazarov's dying words in Turgenev's *Fathers and Sons*—"I have fallen under the wheel"—to foreshadow the tragedy of Jason Edwards.

In his preface to *Under the Wheel* Garland sets the tone for the
work and indicates his political intent:

to present first of all a picture of certain phases of American life, and secon-
darily a problem, because no section of life, carefully considered, fails to
present phases of shortcomings, injustices, and sufferings calculated to
make the thoughtful man fall into deep thought.

For eight years I have been growing steadily in the belief that I have
heard the riddle of the sphinx answered, not by one voice but by many. I
have very definite beliefs as to the line of remedial action but I do not insist
on the infallibility of my belief. I simply say I am satisfied that the destruction of all monopoly in land by a simple governmental levy upon the social
or site-value of the land is the heroic cure for most—if not all—of the dis-
ease and deformity of our social life.

This I have suggested in my play and occasionally in my stories, never I
hope to the great injury of their literary value. I have also aimed at setting
forth in a modest way the growing desire of the modern woman to stand as
an individual beside man.[10]

Garland dedicated the novel to the Farmers' Alliance; and,
although he did not write *Jason Edwards* as Farmers' Alliance
propaganda, he clearly attempted to orient it toward this new
political force which had arisen for the struggle against injustice in
the West.

The novel is divided into two parts. The first part takes place in
Boston in 1884 where Jason Edwards, who had emigrated to the
United States twenty years before, is a mechanic; the second part
takes place five years later, in 1889, in Boomtown where Jason has
moved his family to a farm. In the novel Jason is forced out of
Boston where conditions become unbearable because of reductions
in wages and rises in rent. With his wife and his daughter he
emigrates to the West in search of free land. But he finds that the
land is no longer free, that all of it is in the hands of loan sharks and
speculators, and that he is no better off than he was in Boston. The
high interest leaves Jason penniless and a devastating hailstorm
finally destroys his crops and leaves him paralyzed in his house. His
daughter, Alice, who before had refused to marry Walter Reeves,
eventually gives in and, disillusioned, Jason accepts Walter's
proposal to return to Boston to live with him and Alice.

The basic tension in the novel is the discrepancy between the
promise of the American Dream and what the characters discover.
In it, Garland paints a dismal and oppressive picture of Boston as
lived by the "average man":

Children, ragged, dirty, half-naked and ferocious, swarmed up and down the furnace-like street, swore and screamed in high-pitched, unnatural, animal-like voices, from which all childish music was lost. Frowsy women walking with a gait of utter weariness, aged women, bent and withered, and young women soon to bring other mouths and tongues and hands into this frightful struggle, straggled along the side-walks, laden with parcels, pitifully small, filled with food.[11]

Walter Reeves, newspaper reporter for *The Daily Event* and surrogate-spokesman for Garland, comments on the significance of the scene: "In the thousands of the city, these little mites of humanity have no more significance than toads. They lie here, squat in the way uncared for, and unlovely. What a childhood to look back upon.[12] Although Reeves asserts that "the air is full of revolt against things as they are"[13] and suggests that "man has invented a thousand new ways of producing wealth, but not one for properly distributing it,"[14] he, unlike Garland, never becomes a confirmed advocate of Henry George, whose single-tax theories are expounded in the novel.

When part 2 of the novel opens five years later, we find Jason Edwards trapped in much the same way that he was in Boston. The flight from the city to the country has not resulted in the promised freedom Edwards had hoped for. Free land is too far from the railroad; other land is selling for ten dollars per acre and in the hands of mortgagers; and, whether Edwards is a mechanic or a farmer, he is still a victim. Garland is faithful to history in indicating that the farmers are facing the third season of a drought and short crops. As in Boston, the heat is oppressive and foreboding; but Jason attempts to survive as a farmer, even though everything seems to be conspiring against him—the weather, the prices, his crops, and the men who own the land. Hard work is not enough, however, for his survival.

When it appears that rain will finally come and the storm does arrive, it brings hail. This storm (evidentally the same one we saw in "John Boyle's Conclusion") destroys not only Jason's crops but him physically; and social determinism and fatalism are joined. Jason is not only a victim of a peculiar economic system, but nature also seems to conspire against him. Looking over the destruction, Jason is portrayed as "pathetic, almost to the point of being tragic."[15] And Reeves, in looking over the scene, "could not shake off the feeling that he had been in the presence of a typical American tragedy—the collapse of a working man."[16]

But Garland makes it clear, through Reeves, that it is primarily the economic system and not nature that is responsible. He suggests that Jason is trapped economically on the farm as he was in the city: free land is too far from the railroad; other land is too expensive. Again, Garland advocates the single-tax as a remedy. Nature, however, remains indifferent to man's struggles: "She neither loves nor hates. Her storms have no regard for life. Her smiling calms do not recognize death. Sometimes her storms coincide with death, sometimes her calms run parallel to man's desires. She knows not, and cares nothing."[17]

Despite the fact that there are some powerful moments in the novel, such as the description of the storm which ruins Edwards' crops, Garland's execution of his theme was not skillfully handled. A similar tone and theme were treated much more effectively and dramatically in "Under the Lion's Paw." Garland himself later decided to have the novel excluded from the 1922 edition of his works because it was "too short, too sour of temper, too drab of clothing, too preachy."[18]

Robert Mane suggests that the bleak ending to the novel seems to go against Garland's idealistic vision. But even more inconsistent is the fact that the good nature of most of his characters seems to contradict the tragedy at hand. And at the end (as in *A Spoil of Office*) the loan shark is not so odious as he should be; rather, he seems to be an instrument of relief from suffering. This complicity compromises the moral of the story and indicates that Garland is unable to portray a real villain as he had done earlier with Jim Butler in "Under the Lion's Paw." As a result, *Jason Edwards* becomes neither a simple propagandistic tract nor a real tragedy.[19]

Garland also touches on the theme of women's rights to independence; but Alice Edwards, who carries this theme, is too inadequately developed to do justice to this aspect of the work.

IV   A Member of the Third House

Of Garland's "realistic works," *A Member of the Third House*, which also appeared in 1892, is probably the most disappointing. First written as a play with the same title, the play was never published; but the program of the play indicates that Garland followed the same structure in the novel:

Scene first.—Office of the Duke. "The gutter-snipe must rise."
Scene second.—Water-side. A game of tennis.

Scene third.—A casual call to buy a vote.
Scene fourth.—Committee Room 3. The joint committee sitting.
Scene fifth.—In a *cul de sac*.[20]

Garland's primary theme in *A Member of the Third House* is the political corruption that seems inevitable because of private ownership and monopoly ownership of the land. He moves from a treatment of victims in society of monopoly ownership in *Jason Edwards* to a study of exploiters and political corruption in *A Member of the Third House*. Garland drew heavily for his material upon widely publicized malpractices of railroad companies and upon a particular scandal which had erupted in the Massachusetts legislature in 1890; but he was also inspired by characters from Henrik Ibsen's dramas, particularly Nora and Mrs. Linde from *A Doll's House*.[21]

In the novel Wilson Tuttle, a young intellectual in politics, demands an investigation by a joint committee into the methods of the Consolidated Railway concerning monopolistic practices and bribery of officials in government. The bribery of state officials and lawmakers is carried out principally by a notorious lobbyist, Tom Brennan's and Davis' attorney, Samuel Fox, although the investigation eventually involves the head of the monopoly and father of Helene, with whom Tuttle is in love, the "Iron Duke"—Lawrence B. Davis.

Without proof of bribery and in the absence of support for the investigation, it appears that the investigation will be ineffectual. However, it is saved when Ben Ward, an aging senator, testifies against Davis, even though the testimony brings Ward disgrace. The dilemma of the lovers is resolved when Davis commits suicide, freeing Helene and Tuttle to marry.

Tom Brennan is, in the words of Tuttle, the "real villain, and not a stage caricature."[22] But Garland does present the characters almost as if they are playing a role in a melodramatic production where good and evil are revealed in larger-than-life terms. Brennan is later characterized as "much a product of our society, and especially our government, as the elective railway, or the telephone, or the milk trust. . . . He thinks in 'schemes.' " "His hands clutch money"; he does "not think of himself as a villain"; for "in his world, the ordinary ideas of morality did not apply. He saw his action as a piece of justifiable diplomacy."[23] After bribing Senator Ward, Brennan decides to be a stockholder in Davis' company as well as his son-in-law. He blackmails Davis, threatening to expose him, saying that "the gutter-snipe must rise."

Although characterized as a man of powerful individuality, Davis is portrayed as much as a victim of a corrupt system as he is an exploiter. As the attorney general sums up at the end of the committee hearing, "So long as legislators have the power to vote public values into private pockets the lobby will continue to exist, and its damning work will be seen in the ruin of men like Senator Ward and Mr. Davis, for, as I conceive it, he is a victim of corruption as well as himself being a corrupting agent."[24] Even Brennan says of Davis: "He's a victim of the iridescent dream, as Ingalls calls it."[25]

Ben Ward is a good man, although weak; but his drinking problem contributes as much as anything else to his downfall. In this connection, Robert Mane suggests that, "Instead of an unrelenting satire of political customs, we must ask ourselves if we have only a melodrama of political patronage."[26] If the senator is punished, it is not because he is corrupt but because of his penchant for drink.

As elsewhere, Garland's intrusion into the narrative with commentaries weakens his dramatic force. In the novel he again added Radbourne, a single-tax newspaperman, to advocate his views. He converts Tuttle to his single-tax position so that Tuttle not only is motivated in his investigation by the single-tax influence of Radbourne, but also introduces a bill to levy a graduated increase in annual rent for street privileges.

The novel again indicates the limits of Garland's novelistic method. It lacks the epic breadth Garland was trying to achieve and leaves us merely with a framework. The political environment is simplistic and incomplete; and, because characters are never fully realized, they appear almost unreal at times. And the superficial love story of Helene and Tuttle and the melodramatic suicide of Davis detract from the central conflicts in the novel. Robert Mane suggests, however, that, while the inquest scarcely touches the possibilities of fraud, and the principle behind the practice of lobbying is never questioned, "Several years later an observer could deplore the extraordinary indifference of Americans in regard to corrupt activities. Judged in such a light the novel becomes a good document on the limits of an idealist, an average American, at the end of the last century."[27]

V   A Spoil of Office

Under commission by B. O. Flower, Garland journeyed in 1891 to Kansas, Des Moines, and Washington, D.C., to do an article for the *Arena* on the Farmers' Alliance in Congress and to observe firsthand the agrarian revolt. *A Spoil of Office,* which resulted from his travels, was serialized in the *Arena* from January through June, 1892; and it was published in book length form by the Arena Publishing Company in September, 1892. Despite Garland's later repudiation of the novel as a "partisan plea for a stertorous people's party," Flower was more impressed with this work than he had been with *Jason Edwards* and *A Member of the Third House.*

In *A Spoil of Office,* Garland uses the three principal agrarian movements of the nineteenth century—the Grange, the Farmers' Alliance, and the Populist Party—as a background for tracing the political career of Bradley Talcott, a young Midwesterner, who fervently believes in the goals of the Populist Party. The opening half of the novel deals with Talcott's personal development from a simple farmer into a student at Rock River, and then a lawyer and state legislator. The second half traces his political activities in Des Moines and Washington and relates his growing disilusionment with politics and politicians as an effective means to achieve social ends until he again meets Ida Wilber, a Grange lecturer and crusader for the Farmers' Alliance.

Although Garland purports to use all three agrarian movements in the novel, the story turns sharply before the Populist Party emerges. By detailing the careers of Bradley and Ida, Garland was able to suggest an accurate picture of the progress of the farmer's movement from the Grange to the People's Party and to suggest the evolution of minds and growing political awareness which made such a transition possible. Later, in speaking about the novel, Garland explained his intention:

The idea in *The Spoil of Office* was to treat the West and its great political movements and revolutions as they would stand related to a young man of political ambitions like Bradley Talcott. The whole book deals with things and events as seen from this young man's center. I tried to take him through a development of a farm hand whose opportunities had been meager and who did not realize his power of development, on through many changes, up to his life in congress—that is, to apparent success.

His success, however, consisted in his keeping himself clean and unspotted in his public life, so full of temptations. The climax of his life . . . .

came in his rise to a comprehension of the altruism which was expressed
throughout by Ida Wilber. While it is a political novel, it is a political novel
as the veritist would make it.[28]

As in his other economic novels, Garland traces economic suffering to the effects of monopoly. He indicates that "There is no war
between the town and the country—the war is between the people
and the monopolist wherever he is, whether he is in the country or
in the town."[29] But, while Garland is convinced of the necessity for
reform, he also recognizes the obstacle of uniting the poor and
effecting meaningful social change. In fact, the title suggests
Garland's sentiment relative to futility and to his awareness of
failure. Garland recognizes the extent of corruption in the political
process and the indecisiveness of Bradley in the novel gives us an
insight into Garland's political views—his rejection and suspicion of
political processes and his confusion about how to deal with
agrarian problems. Clearly, by 1892, Garland had become sufficiently disillusioned about the direction of the Populist Party as
not to share Ida Wilber's enthusiasm when she said: "I hope to see
our reform established before the grey comes into my hair. It will be
accomplished if we are true to ourselves; if our leaders are true to
themselves; if they do not become spoils of office. . . ; if they are
true to their best convictions, and speak the new thoughts that come
to them."[30]

As with the two previous novels, A Spoil of Office again shows
Garland's limitations as a novelist. He is strongest when dealing
with agrarian material he knew well; but, when he moves to the city, he becomes superficial. His characters again are not sufficiently
developed to enable Garland to dramatize the conflict between
them or within Bradley himself. Although Garland occasionally introduces important issues, such as the economic implications of
feminism and the plight of the farmer's wife, and indicates that
"they are today the most terrible proofs of man's inhumanity,"[31] his
plot fails to present them with dramatic force. Despite all of these
failures as a novel, however, A Spoil of Office still remains an excellent piece of social history because it provides insights into the
dilemmas facing the farmer during the late nineteenth century and
of the parties that developed during a period of reform.

CHAPTER 5

Toward Romanticism

I   *The Search for Literary Acceptance*

IN January, 1894, Garland announced that he was renouncing all controversial literature in favor of purely literary works.[1] While what he meant by this statement is open to speculation, it seems clear that, while Garland continued to treat such controversial social themes as woman's rights in marriage and the plight of the American Indian, he no longer focused on controversial economic fiction as he had done in *Jason Edwards, A Member of the Third House, A Spoil of Office,* and in some of his earlier short fiction. He would, in other words, choose the road offered to him by Gilder rather than by B. O. Flower who was influential in encouraging him to use his art as an instrument of social protest. In fact, Garland had made this decision a couple of years earlier; and while, as I have indicated, Garland felt this tension from the beginning, it was not until after 1892 that Garland consciously decided to cease embodying political and economic ideas in his fiction.

Three works in particular illustrate his new style set against his economic ficition: *A Little Norsk,* "Land of the Saddle-bug," and *Rose of Dutcher's Coolly.* The imporance of these works lies less in their time of publication as in Garland's choice of the main character and the themes. In each of these works Garland assigns the principal role to a heroine, and he develops a concern for woman which has been found in his earlier fiction. But he does not, as he had done earlier, simply treat the plight of the farm wife; he puts the female's problem into a larger context: the role of women in modern society, and the necessity of equality in marriage.

While Garland studied each of his characters in relation to the society in which he was placed, his characters became more important than the plot. Garland evinced with them his development of idealism; for he indicates that, by the extension of the individual will, the average human being can become unusual; that man is not placed in a deterministic universe in which he cannot prevail. Thus while Garland presented a social study, he was optimistic about man's possibilities.

II A Little Norsk

A *Little Norsk*, a short novelette, first appeared as "Ol' Pap's Flaxen" in the *Century* for March, April, and May, 1892. However, the work, which had been written in 1888, was accepted by Gilder in 1892; but it was held in reserve for more than two years before Gilder finally published it. While the novel was still appearing in the *Century*, Garland sold the book rights to D. Appleton and Company under the new title. This work, which grew out of Garland's experience in Dakota in 1883, was his first romantic novel. The novel relates how Ans Wood and Bert Gearheart, two bachelors holding down a claim during a Dakota blizzard (much like Garland himself had done), took care of Elga (Flaxen), a small Norwegian girl of five, whose parents had frozen to death in a snowstorm. The two men raise her until they resolve to send her to college in Minnesota. Although both men love her, she falls in love with and marries a young scoundrel, Will Kendall. However, after she has a child, Kendall dies and Elga returns to Ans and Bert. The novel closes with the suggestion that she will marry Gearheart.

The realism of Dakota farm life is presented effectively and vividly, and Garland's treatment of Flaxen's development is handled sensitively. As Robert Mane suggests, the pioneers experience total solidarity, and possess both courage and an immense capacity for resistance against the cold and the heat and the rough life on the prairie.[2] The story suffers, however, from the conventional sentimental ending and from the artificiality of the plot. In his original version, for example, Garland had sanctioned a divorce between Will and Flaxen, but he decided in a rewritten version to insert an accidental death to resolve the problem of a bad marriage. As Donald Pizer suggests, *A Little Norsk* reveals Garland's basic incapacity to develop successful plots in his longer fiction: "The material he could handle with force and brilliance—the single-minded dramatization of highly charged moral indignation as the representation of the commonality of middle-border life—he could rarely expand beyond the shorter fictional forms."[3]

III The Moccasin Ranch

More successful than *A Little Norsk* was Garland's novelette
"The Land of the Straddle-Bug" which appeared serially in the
Chap-Book from November 15, 1894, to February 15, 1895. and
which was later reissued as *The Moccasin Ranch* (1909). In this
work Garland is able to integrate a compelling moral idea with
forceful action and with a striking and meaningful setting. The
story is set in Dakota during 1883 - 1884; and the settlers, who are
silhouetted against the landscape, are coming to the "land of the
straddle-bug" to stake a claim:

> The settlers came like locusts; they sang like larks. From Alsace and
> Lorraine, from the North Sea, from Russia, from the Alps, they came, and
> their faces shone as if they had happened upon the spring-time of the
> world. Tyranny was behind them, the majesty of God's wilderness before
> them, a mystic joy within them.
> Under their hands the straddle-bug multiplied. He is short lived, this
> prairie insect. He usually dies in thirty-days—by courtesy alone he lives. He
> expresses the settlers' hope and sense of justice. In the spring days of good
> cheer he lived at times sixty days—but only on strong ground or fire-
> scarred, peaty lowlands.
> He withered—this strange, three-legged, voiceless insect—but in his
> stead arose a bettle. This beetle sheltered human beings, and was called a
> shack.[4]

Against this background, Garland tells the story of Blanche and
Howard Burke who leave Boomtown in early spring for McPherson
County to stake a claim; they are accompanied by Jim Rivers and
Robert Bailey, who plan to open a general store.

Each chapter not only has the name of a month—beginning with
May and ending in December—and corresponds to the cycle of the
seasons but reflects the movement of the novel's characters from enthusiasm to anxiety and depression. The joyous, productive spring is
followed by a hot, dry summer and finally by a severe, bitter winter.

Blanche's restlessness and her isolation in particular begins in late
autumn and leads to an illicit affair with Jim Rivers. By late winter,
she is pregnant; and she and Rivers decide to flee. Instead of ending
the story at this point, as he had in "A Branch Road" where Will
and Agnes escape over the mountains, Garland explores their situation by forcing them to come to terms with and to justify their actions. Caught in a blizzard, they are forced to stop at Bailey's store

until the storm has subsided; and Bailey, who initially is shocked by the apparent immorality of their actions, resolves to prevent their leaving. But he slowly comes not only to sympathize with Blanche's plight, but to understand how their actions do not conform to conventional morals. As he struggles, he begins to see that

> It made social conventions of no value, and narrowed the question of morality to the relationship of these three human souls.
> Lying there in the dark, with the elemental war of wind and snow filling the illimitable arch of sky, he came to feel, in a dim, wordless way, that this tragedy was born of conventions largely. Also it appeared infinitesimal, like the activities of insects battling, breeding, dying. He came also to feel that the force which moved these human insects, was akin to the ungovernable sweep of the wind and snow—all inexplicable, elemental, unmoral.[5]

But Garland prevents a tragedy by having all of the participants resolve, in their own way, to defy convention. Bailey finally decides to leave the decision to Blanche; and, when she chooses to leave with Rivers, he happily sends them on their way.

In this novelette Garland was therefore able not only to expose the social problem of women's rights but also to dramatize the conflicts between a naturalistic view of man and his environment (illustrated, for example, in the abundant use of insect imagery), romantic individualism, and traditional morality.

IV   Rose of Dutcher's Coolly

Published in 1895 and revised in 1899, *Rose of Dutcher's Coolly* is Garland's most ambitious and generally his best full-length novel. The idea for the novel first occurred to him during the winter of 1890 - 1891 while he was on a lecture tour in the Midwest and made some notes for a prospective short story to be called "A Father's Love":

> Story of a man whose only child, girl, started to school from a narrow valley. How her mind expanded and her home narrowed.
> The father, seeing he was losing her, tried to make home so pleasant she could stay at home. He bought new furniture, built a new house while she was away at school.
> Watched her anxiously, silently.
> She was made all the more miserable. It made her seem like a criminal but she couldn't stay in the valley.

He went into La Crosse with her. Went East with her to a New England conservatory. At last she meets a fine man and marries him.[6]

Garland worked on the novel intermittently from 1890 to 1895. Begun as a short story, it was developed into a novelette in 1893, and finally expanded to novel length by 1895. As Donald Pizer suggests, the themes grow more numerous and complex as the length of the work increased. While the novel initially intended to focus on traditional family conflicts between youthful horizons and familial roots, it gradually began to include also the nature and role of modern woman and an illustration of Garland's theories of art that he had previously expounded in *Crumbling Idols* in 1894. The latter half of the novel particularly concerns Garland's views on the nature of true art, the social injustices of the double standard, and the subservient role of women within marriage.[7]

Garland changed slightly his original plan for the narrative by bringing Rose to the University of Wisconsin in Madison to complete her education and by then taking her to Chicago, rather than to New England, to discover herself as a writer and as an individual. The change was probably influenced by Garland's belief that Chicago was increasingly becoming a vital center for the arts and by his personal experiences there that had confirmed that view. In Chicago Rose finally decides to marry Warren Mason, a worldly newspaperman; for she has learned that freedom and marriage are not incompatible.

The construction of the plot remains fairly simple, but the characters rather than the plot hold our dominant interest. Moreover, the moral, social, intellectual, and sexual development of Rose herself is most absorbing. A sizable portion of the novel not only deals with Rose's discovery that freedom and marriage are not incompatible but with Garland's wish to emphasize through her development that sexual knowledge and experience are inseparable when one grows up on a farm, and that such knowledge can be a source of moral and social development rather than, as in Theodore Dreiser's *Sister Carrie*, or in Stephen Crane's *Maggie: A Girl of the Streets*, a cause of social catastrophe.[8] Garland traces Rose's development from her first sexual awakening and shows that a woman who possessed vitality, willpower, and moral strength could triumph over sexual desire and a depressing environment, and develop intellectually without losing her femininity.

While Garland was always a romantic individualist to a degree, his early stories often portray man as a victim of forces beyond his control. In *Rose* Garland clearly disregards the strong environmental determinism found in his earlier material. To be sure, Rose is influenced by forces from both within and without, and much of her success is dependent on an element of chance, but Garland's faith in individual strength and in the freedom of will is much stronger than we find either in Crane or Dreiser or in Garland's earlier material.

As Lars Ahnebrink points out, Crane's purpose in *Maggie* (first published in 1893) was, among other things, to show the malevolence of all men and the indifferent and negative attitude of society to the individual whose ruin was of no consequence to it. While Maggie is described as innocent and as possessing inherent goodness, her ruin is nevertheless inevitable because of the environmental and social forces against which the individual could do little.[9] In speaking of *Maggie*, Crane wrote in an inscribed number of copies which he sent to friends in 1893: "It is inevitable that you will be greatly shocked by this book but continue please with all possible courage to the end. For it trys to show that environment is a tremendous thing in the world and frequently shapes lives regardless. If one proves that theory one makes room in Heaven for all shorts of souls (notably an occasional street girl) who are not confidently expected to be there by many excellent people."[10] While Garland was impressed by a number of things in *Maggie* such as its style, sincerity, truthfulness, directness, dialect, and lack of convention in the treatment of the slums, he nevertheless felt that "the story fails of rounded completeness. It is only a fragment. It is typical only of the worst elements of the alley. The author should delineate the families living on the next street, who live lives of heroic purity and hopeless hardships."[11]

While both *Maggie* and *Rose* treat sexual themes, the manner in which the authors treat such material is handled differently. In *Maggie*, the theme itself shocked readers, for Crane was less concerned with Maggie's sexual awareness than he was with forces outside which ruined her. Garland's readers were also shocked by *Rose*, but for different reasons. Garland's readers confused his treatment of Rose's sexual development by misinterpreting Garland's intention, viewing his portrayal of Rose as an emphasis upon merely base animal sexuality. Garland was shocked by the reaction to the novel (some reviewers even felt it should be banned) since he felt he had been careful to illustrate that Rose's sexuality benefitted from her personal and her social restraints.

To be sure, Garland, like Dreiser, associated sex with a force in nature; but, unlike Dreiser, Garland wanted Rose's sexuality to be viewed in a larger moral context. Garland basically rejected the essence of naturalism which held the conviction that society must be seen entirely as a force of nature. While Rose is closely identified with nature, especially early in the novel, her control over those forces sets her apart from the determinism found among the naturalistic writers. Thus, when Rose is accosted on the train to Madison by a leering brakeman, whom Garland refers to as a "sex-maniac," he wishes us to be as revolted by his behavior as Rose was. When Carrie Meeber, on the other hand, is approached by the drummer, Drouet, we accept the incident as natural and do not condemn either Carrie or Drouet for their subsequent actions.[12] And, while both Rose and Carrie are attracted to a number of men, Garland's and Dreiser's beliefs in the efficacy of free will, human freedom, and moral restraint are clearly different.

This view is reinforced when, a number of years later, Garland indicated his dissatisfaction with the treatment of sex in modern literature. He remarked in 1934 that "We are sex-mad from my point of view—but I am aware that these incidents are considered necessary in an advanced literature. To me—as an evolutionist—they are a return to the life of the animals who are supposed to be lower on the scale of life."[13] Furthermore, he was particularly displeased to be linked with Dreiser, which he indicated in a letter to Carl Van Doren:

I appreciate the very great compliment involved in your mentioning me in your lectures as one of the sidelines. I am grateful for any remembrance now [1920]—but I do not see how you can find any connection between Dreiser and myself. I am an old fogy. I believe in marriage, the home, prohibition, censorship, the single tax and many other isms that are now discredited by the "young" writers of fifty. I have always hated obscenity, tales of vice and crime, and jokes about the chastity or modesty of women. I have never written about vice or crime. My stories are hard and rude and sordid but not in the beastly sense. I have never held with the pornographic school and my most advanced notions in "Crumbling Idols," as you know, had nothing to do with the glorification of sexual promiscuity. I am an individualist but my notions of liberty do not include license. . . . It is so easy to write stories of sexual "irregularites." I have tried to keep close to the normal, decent, hard-working folk of my day.[18]

Garland was careful to distinguish between the glorification of sexual promiscuity and sexual "irregularities" of the "pornographic writers" and the natural emotional development of Rose which was held in check by moral and social restraints.

We follow Rose's emotional and intellectual development basically through three major phases, upon which the novel is structured: her early years on the farm, her college years at the University of Wisconsin at Madison, and finally her development into full maturity in Chicago. Within this larger structure, however, each chapter corresponds closely to a particular phase in her development.

In the first part of the novel, we are exposed to the realities of youthful sexual experience. In a chapter entitled "Dangerous Days" Rose is awakened to the realities of sexual experiences quite naturally:

> A farmer's daughter is exposed to sights and sounds which the city girl knows nothing of. Mysterious processes of generation and birth go on before the eyes of a farm child, which only come as obscene whisperings to the city child of the same middle condition and these happenings have a terrifying power to stir and develop passions prematurely. . . . She learned early the hideous signs which pass in the country to describe the unnamable and covert things of human life. She saw them scrawled on the fences, on the school-house doors, and written on the dust of the road. There was no escaping them. The apparently shameful fact of sex faced her everywhere.[15]

But Garland tells us that, although Rose had experienced firsthand courtship, birth, and death, "through it all she lived a glad, free, and wholesome life."[16]

Her first sexual encounter occurs before the age of fifteen when she finds herself alone with Carl, her first "love":

> She felt a terrible hunger, a desire to take his head in her arms and kiss it. Her muscles ached and quivered with something she could not fathom. As she resisted she grew calm, but mysteriously sad, as if something were passing from her forever. The leaves whispered a message to her, and the stream repeated an occult note of joy, which was mixed with sorrow.
>
> The struggle of wild fear and bitter-sweet hunger of desire—this vague, mystical perception of her sex, did not last, to Rose. It was lost when she came out of the woods into the road on the way homeward.[17]

For Rose, this encounter was the "second great epoch of her life,"[18] but the first one had been the death of her mother and the subsequent intrusion of her aunt into her life to help her father rear her when she was very young. We remain, unfortunately, unenlightened about what the details of the relationship with Carl were, but we suspect that Rose is merely guilty of some youthful petting. Wisely John Dutcher, upon discovery of the act, merely scolds the "lovers"; for he considers the whole episode an act of youthful indiscretion.

Rose's attentions are then directed to William DeLisle, a circus performer, whose presence overwhelms her at the performance which she attends with a group of other children. In several hours of the performance, Rose is overcome by the "luminous beauty" of the acrobat's half-nude body. But, psychologically, the performer represents much more to Rose; his image of physical strength and artistic success is the ideal which captures Rose's imagination; and, thereafter, he becomes for Rose a symbol of the vast ambitions which would occupy her thoughts increasingly and which could not be accomplished on the farm.

On the farm we follow Rose through her first knowledge of sex as she observes farm life, as she runs naked through the corn fields and is fascinated by the nudity of boys swimming, as she has her first encounter with sex, and as she develops her idealization of sexual power in the acrobat. That this knowledge was not a morally corrupting influence is indicated by Rose's revulsion when she is approached by the brakeman on the way to Madison when she decides to leave the farm. At the university sexual urges exist, but Rose is able to keep her emotions in check:

> Something elemental stirred in her blood as the leaves came out. The young men took on added grace and power in her eyes. When they came before her in their athletic suits, lithe, clean-limbed, joyous, then her eyes dreamed and her heart beat till the blood choked her breathing.
>
> O, the beautiful sky, O, the shine and shade of leaves! O, the splendors of young manhood! She fought down the dizziness which came to her. She smiled mechanically as they stood before her with frank, clear eyes and laughing lips, and so, slowly, brain reasserted itself over flesh, and she, too, grew frank and gay.[19]

While we know very little of her actual life in Madison, Rose develops intellectually, nearly falls in love twice, but resists; and she begins to set goals for herself which she feels could not be gained if she gave herself to marriage and motherhood. As Robert Mane has shown, if there are occasions when Rose is "tormented," it is by the idea of sex or the flesh more than the flesh itself. All the battles unfold in her imagination.[20]

Intellectually, she grapples with such questions as freedom, marriage, motherhood, and the rights of women. And even her reading reinforces her resistance to giving in to her instincts, for she is powerfully moved by Hawthorne's *The Scarlet Letter*, "rebelling against the insatiable vengeance of the populace who condemned Hester as if she had opened the gate of hell in the path of every daughter of New England. She could not understand, then nor thereafter, the ferocity of hate which went out against the poor defenseless woman."[21]

But, through all her tests, Garland clearly indicates that not only were there intellectual restraints but that, in the most trying moments of her life,

some hidden force rose up to dominate the merely animal forces within. Some organic magnificent inheritance of moral purity. She was saved by forces within, not by laws without. Opportunities to sin are always offered in every life. Virtue is not negative, it is positive; it is a decoration won by fighting, resisting. This sweet and terrible attraction of men and women towards each other is as natural and as moral as the law of gravity, and as inexorable. Its perversion produces trouble. Love must be good and fine and according to nature, else why did it give such joy and beauty?[22]

After graduation (the account of which Garland relates with particular effectiveness), Rose returns to the farm for the summer. But she realizes that, although her father has refurnished the house in her honor and expects her to live with him, she must leave the farm if she is to achieve her goals. While Garland makes it clear that farm life would stifle Rose's ambitions, he does not deal with the depressing aspects of the farm nearly as much as he does in his earlier fiction. Rather, he deals with this problem psychologically from Rose's point of view, although the limited opportunities of a farm wife were well know to Garland's readers.

The last section of the novel which takes Rose to Chicago is important to the theme, but it lacks the freshness and the spontaneity of the earlier sections and suffers from being too talkative. While Rose continues her intellectual and social development, Garland seems equally concerned with expounding his views about women's rights and the nature of true art.

When Rose first arrives in Chicago, Garland attempts to evoke the enormous power and terror of the city: "Tensions thickened. Smells assaulted her sensitive nostrils, uncomprehensible and horrible odors. Everywhere men delved in dirt and murk, and all un-

loveliness. Streets began to stretch away on either side, inter-
minable, squalid, filled with scowling, squaw-like women and elfish
children. The darkness grew, making the tangle and tumult a dead-
ly struggle." In her reaction to the city, Rose wonders "Was this the
city of her dream? This the magnificent, the home of education and
art."[23]

Rose, who is prepared to meet the challenge the city offers, imag-
ines that she is in the midst of a human drama, in the center of
human life: "So it was—the wonderful and the terrifying appealed
to her mind first. In all the city she saw the huge and fierce. She
perceived only contrasts. She saw the ragged newsboy and the
towering policeman. She saw the ragpickers, the street vermin, with
a shudder of pity and horror, and she saw also the gorgeous show
windows of the great stores. . . . It all seemed a battlefield. There
was no hint of repose."[24]

But unlike Carrie Meeber's experience in Chicago, Rose is never
really forced to confront the horrible and terrifying aspects of the city. Rose is introduced to an aspiring and intellectual group of
writers, artists, and professional people; and in this circle she usually spends her time and meets Warren Mason, a worldly Chicago
newspaperman. Under Warren's influence, Rose develops from an
imitative to an original writer. Her repudiation of conformity and
imitation in literature closely follows Garland's attitudes toward art
that he was widely espousing, but such views are also consistent
with Rose's desire for individuality.

With her intellectual and artistic development secure, Rose must
finally come to terms with her conflicting desires for freedom and
marriage. While confronted with the opportunity to marry the
wealthy Elbert Harvey, but really desiring Warren, Rose witnesses a
storm on Lake Michigan that is one of Garland's most skillful uses
of natural incidents. The storm is magnificently described and
parallels Rose's internal storm. Rose, who in the company with
Mason, had gone to the lake shore to see the spectacle is completely
overcome by Harvey. Harvey takes her to see his family and an
engagement is almost concluded. However, the inspiring effect of
the storm on Mason, which included the heroism of a Negro rescuing three shipwrecked persons, affects Rose.

After Rose returns to the farm, Warren's letter of proposal
reaches her and convinces her that she can have both marriage and
personal freedom, for he writes: "I want you as a comrade and
lover, not as a subject or servant, or unwilling wife. I do not claim

any rights over you at all. You can bear me children or not, just as you please. You are a human soul like myself, and I shall expect you to be as free and as sovereign as I, to follow any profession or do any work which pleases you."[25]

Rose's transformation from the wild, elflike girl on the farm to the sophisticated New Woman is thus completed; not only, as her name suggests, has she "risen" in society, but she has blossomed into a cultivated flower.

With the exception of Rose and Mason, Garland's characters remain generally static and serve as the background influences against which Rose's development can be seen and measured. Carl, her first love, is full of youthful physical passion, but he remains trapped at the threshold of maturity. William DeLisle is never really portrayed beyond the image which Rose has of him. Dr. Thatcher, who is instrumental in convincing Rose to leave the farm for the university, provides a home for her for a period of time. However, recognizing that he is falling in love with his young protégé, he nobly decides that she must leave. Likewise the minor female characters, who are also involved in Rose's development, remain static; for Garland was not sufficiently interested in their lives to do much with their characters despite the fact that it was technically necessary to develop them more.

Rose's father, John Dutcher, while also fairly static, is more absorbing. Garland handles his treatment of Dutcher's struggle to rear Rose without a mother with particular sensitivity. And his internal struggle between his desire, which urges him to fight to keep Rose, and his intellect, which tells him he must let her go, is particularly moving. When Rose leaves the farm for the first time to attend the university, he discreetly resigns himself to his fate. But his expectations are momentarily raised when Rose returns from Chicago after her announced engagement. At the end, however, in a moving and poignant scene, John Dutcher, seated near his beehives with his face in his hands, weeps for his lost daughter.

If the novel occasionally suffers from a lack of execution, particularly the artificial contrivances of plot in the second half of the novel, it generally succeeds in combining a compelling theme with the power of description and lyrical simplicity characteristic of the best short stories of Garland's early years.

V   Wayside Courtships

In February, 1897, Garland signed a contract with D. Appleton and Company for a reissue *A Spoil of Office*, which had been released to him by Stone and Kimball, and for a new volume of collected short stories to be entitled *Wayside Courtships*. For this volume Garland collected eleven stories of uneven lengths and diversity of theme, most of which had previously appeared in journals between 1888 and 1897.[26] These stories, while including a variety of themes, deal with the relations of men and women, and serve, in many ways, as companion pieces to *Main-Travelled Roads* and *Prairie Folks*. Although the title of the volume suggests a collection of romances, several stories that deal with the harsher side of love give his theme of the treatment of love more complexity and, on the whole, more strength.

The main stories are contained between an opening vignette, "At the Beginning," which briefly depicts two young lovers full of youthful romance moved emotionally by the sight and presence of each other at an opera, and a concluding piece, "The End of Love is Love of Love," which portrays an old married couple who are resting on a beach after life has driven the romance from their marriage. The elderly man wants to forget that he is old and timid and that youthful romanticism and love are gone. He urges his wife to forget and help him forget the intervening years:

He could not understand her. He did not try. He lay with closed eyes, tired, purposeless. The sweet sea wind touched his cheek, white with the indoor pallor of the desk worker. The sound of the sea exalted him. The beautiful clouds above him carried him back to boyhood. There were tears on his face as he looked up at her.

"I'm forgetting!" he said, with a smile of exaltation.

But the woman looked away at the violet-shadowed sails, afar on the changeful purple of the sea, and her throat choked with pain.[27]

Unlike the characters we meet in either *Main-Travelled Roads* or *Prairie Folks*, we do not find the main characters on the farm; rather, we usually meet them, generally college bred, on the train either going to or passing through a small town. In the first story, "A Preacher's Love Story," we encounter Wallace Stacey, who is just out of college and who is on his way by train to Illinois to look for a position as a preacher and teacher. He gets a position in Cyene through a man he meets on the train, Herman Allen, a cynical, worldly college dropout who intends to make his fortune on the Wheat Exchange in Chicago. Stacey, a Baptist, intends to stay with Herman; but after he meets Herman's sister Mattie the latter's father, a comfirmed Methodist, learns of Stacey's religion and asks him to leave the house.

Stacey finds the church run down; and, because of the religious divisions, he is offered no help by either the Methodists or Baptists to rebuild it. However, he resolves to rebuild the church; and, after a series of inspirational sermons, he brings everyone together, including Mattie's father. When Stacey becomes ill, the town rebuilds the church; he falls in love with Mattie; and the story ends with their anticipated marriage. A romantic story, it suggests the unity of all people and the power of love. But the story has poor dramatization, is overly sentimental, and is weak in depicting local color.

Like "A Preacher's Love Story," romance penetrates "A Meeting in the Foothills." In this narrative, Arthur Ramsey, also a college graduate, arrives in Red Rock by train looking for a foreman's position at a dairy farm. After searching in vain, he finally accepts a position as a common hand with wealthy Major Thayer. Thoroughly chauvinistic, Arthur is angered by the major's British partner, Saulisbury, who makes him feel like a servant or butler. Eventually, however, Ramsey is able to win Edith, the major's niece, and to convince everyone that he is more than a commoner. Again, the story ends with the promise of marriage; but it lacks sufficient tension, dramatization, and development of character to carry the theme. Already in these two stories we get a glimpse of the sentimentalism and romance which will appear throughout several novels to follow.

"A Stop-over at Tyre" is a more successful story, and it also has closer ties with the best stories in *Main-Travelled Roads* than do the previous two. Albert Lohr, a student who is working as a book agent to earn enough money to get back to school, is on a train trip when he receives a telegram from his friend Jim Hartley to stop at Tyre. Arriving in town in the middle of the night during a storm, he is pursuaded by Hartley to stay for a short time to help him work the territory as a book agent before returning to school. He meets Maud, Mrs. Welch's daughter, at the boardinghouse where they are staying. Like Rose Dutcher, Maud longs to leave the small town and return to school; however, her responsibility to take care of her mother prevents her doing so. Despite Maud's breaking of her engagement with her jealous fiancé, Bert decides he must leave during the spring and return to school without her. However, he is so in love with Maud that he finally decides to marry her, although his marriage will probably mean that he will never return to school and fulfill his ambitions.

Hartley, who is unhappy about Bert's decision, feels partially responsible for it: "Like most men in America, and especially Western men, he [Hartley] still clung to the idea that a man was entirely responsible for his success or failure in life. He had not admitted that conditions of society might be so adverse that only men of most exceptional endowments, and willing and able to master many of the best and deepest and most sacred of their inspirations and impulses, could succeed."[28] Bert recognizes his dilemma precisely, however, and knows what his decision will mean: "As long as his love-dreams went out toward a vague and ideal woman, supposedly higher and grander than himself, he was spurred on to face the terrible sheer escapement of social eminence; but when he met, by sheer accident, the actual woman who was to inspire his future efforts, the difficulties he faced took on solid reality."[29] But Hartley can only conclude that Bert has "jumped into a hole and pulled the hole in after him."[30]

The story effectively depicts the tensions involved in Bert's loss of ambition and aspiration because of his marriage, but it also discloses a greater skepticism concerning the possibilities of romantic love than the two previous stories. However, not everything in marriage is similarly delightful. In "Alien in the Pines," we are confronted by a man who calls himself Williams who was formerly a talented violinist but who works as a woodcutter in the pines in Wisconsin. Destroyed by drink, he left his family; but he sent part of his check to it each month for its welfare. However, at the end of the story a burst of shame overcomes him, and he decides to return to his wife to try to make their marriage a successful one.

In "The Owner of the Mill Farm," Garland focuses on brutality and jealousy which have consequences as disastrous as drunkenness. The central character is a young student named Morris who goes to the Mill Farm of Tom and Minnie Miner to fix the barn roof. Because a total breakdown in communication between Tom and Minnie has clearly occurred, Morris eventually sympathizes with Minnie. As the owner of the farm, she has never wanted to part with it. Her husband, whom she married against her parent's wishes, has never let her forget it and has continually brutalized her ever since she made an indiscreet remark. Morris, enraged over Tom's behavior, provokes a fight, subdues him, and makes him repent to his wife. The remedy, however, is only temporary; for, when Morris returns to college, affairs return to pretty much what they had been before his intervention. In this story, the tone remains somber throughout, setting it apart from most of the stories in the volume.

In "Of Those Who Seek," the same young man reappears in four separate vignettes. In the first piece, he notices a young Indian girl who is deaf, dumb, and blind. He perceives that, having "the prisoned soul," her life must remain a cruel fragment, imprisoned in darkness. In the next piece, while running for political office, he envies the sheltered life of a rich, well-protected girl. She, on the other hand, longs to be released from her humdrum existence and to join him in his struggle. Both idealize the other's way of life, and each is dissatisfied with his own.

When we next see him in "A Fair Exile," he is on a train on the way to Boomtown; and he overhears a story by a young woman who had gone through a difficult childhood with a coarse father and who is now in the midst of a divorce from a drunken, dissolute man. Now she is alone, with only sympathetic observers. But, in "The Passing Stranger," Garland indicates that redemption is always possible for lost souls. The young man passes by an infamous bar in New York where he sees a young woman. When she sees him, she feels herself compelled to leave the bar and return to her village. This piece is much more mystical than any of the others in the volume.

In his next story, "Before the Low Green Door" (see Chapter 3 for a full discussion of the story), Garland depicts the broken farm wife, Matilda Bent, who is dying from cancer. The tone of this story, which was first published in 1887 as "A Common Case," is utterly antiromantic and is a contrast with the dominant positive tone of the volume. Garland then ends the volume with a more idyllic story, "Upon Impulse," in which Mr. Jenkins Ware, a lawyer, becomes infatuated at a social gathering with Miss Powell, a teacher. Reminding him of a schoolteacher he once idolized, he has an impulse to ask her to marry him. After hesitating about accepting his proposal, she finally agrees to follow her impulses and feelings and not to rationalize them. The story ends with an implication that they will be married.

After *Wayside Courtships*, and after putting in abeyance his projected biography of Grant, Garland left the middle-border and turned to the Mountain West for his material. Except for his autobiographical *Boy Life on the Prairie* (1899), he did not return to middle-border fiction until much later when he dealt with this material in a number of autobiographies.

CHAPTER 6

The High Country

I *A Turn to the Mountain West*

WHILE Garland's turn to the Mountain West for his material signaled a change in those subjects with which he had been occupied in his middle-border fiction, the shift was not an abrupt one. While still at work on *Rose of Dutcher's Coolly*, he was beginning to meditate on themes connected with Colorado; and, though he did not at once begin writing about Western material, a trip to Colorado was the beginning of his career as writer of Mountain West fiction. As Garland later recalled, "From the plains, which were becoming each year more crowded, more prosaic, I fled in imagination as in fact to the looming silver-and-purple summits of the Continental Divide, while in my mind an ambition to embody, as no one at that time had done, the spirit and the purpose of the Rocky Mountain trailer was vaguely forming in my mind."[1] So, even before Garland's second visit to the West in 1895, he was psychologically prepared to look elsewhere for his material.

When *Rose of Dutcher's Coolly* was attacked as savagely as *Main-Travelled Roads* had been, Garland had also become depressed: "With a foolish notion that the Middle West should take a moderate degree of pride in me, I resented this condemnation. . . . Without doubt this persistent antagonism, this almost universal depreciation of my stories of the Plains had something to do with intensifying the joy with which I returned to the mountain world and its heroic types, at any rate I spent July and August of that year [1895] in Colorado and New Mexico, making many observations, which turned out to have incalculable value to me in later days."[2] This trip marked what Garland called "a complete 'bout face in my march," for it provided him with material for *The Eagle's Heart*, *Witches' Gold*, *Money Magic*, and a dozen shorter romances.[3]

80

But although Garland dreamed of the "High Country," his biography, *Ulysses Grant: His Life and Character,* absorbed most of his time between 1895 and 1897. Not until June, 1897, when Garland took a tour which began with a study of the Sioux at Standing Rock, did he devote himself entirely to Western material. During the next several months he lived with his brother among the Sioux, Crow, and Cheyenne. He remarked that:

This trip completed my conversion. I resolved to preempt a place in the history of the great Northwest which was at once a wilderness and a cosmopolis, for in it I found men and women from many lands, drawn to the mountains in search of health, or recreation, or gold. I perceived that almost any character I could imagine could be verified in this amazing mixture. I began to sketch novels which would have been false in Wisconsin or Iowa. With a sense of elation, of freedom, I decided to swing out into the wider air of Colorado and Montana.[4]

In his new material Garland attempted to deal with a variety of facets of Western life and to create a multiplicity of types, but he usually focused on mountaineers, miners, foresters, and Indians. With few exceptions, most of his works during this period contain common elements: mild social themes, a sense of the glory of mountain scenery, and a conventional love plot. Most of the works were derived from Garland's travels during this period, whether his gold mining expedition to Alaska (recounted in *Trail of the Gold Seekers*), his journey to England (recorded in *Her Mountain Lover*), or his trips to Indian reservations (in *The Book of the American Indian* and *Captain of the Gray Horse Troop*).

II The Eagle's Heart

The Eagle's Heart (1900), Garland's "Colorado Novel," became one of the first fruits of his Western travels; but this work is also the central one among his romantic novels because Garland attempted to put everything into it: the scene, the technique, the conventions, and, most of all, the types of characters that were to form the basis of his other Western novels. The novel illustrates his new style and concerns, and it also exemplifies both his strengths and, ultimately, his failure as a Romantic novelist.

The simple plot of the novel, which contains little complication, has one major purpose: to record the adventures, aspirations, and development of its hero, Harold Excell. The action takes place in three sections. In the first section, Harold is presented as a boy in the small farming community of Rock River, where his father is a minister. Known even early in his life for his furious temper in which "he scared his opponents by the suddenness and the intensity of his rage, which was fairly demonical in fury,"[5] the boy's angry temperament makes him a rebel and a desperado · and is a characteristic which he must continually fight. Recalling Rose Dutcher, there is a persistent tension between his base instincts and his high aspirations.

But, when he is seventeen, he is unable to hold his temper in check and is involved in a fight in which he stabs Clint Slocum in self-defense. He is nonetheless found guilty and sentenced to six months in the county jail. After his release from jail, he changes his name to Moses N. Hardluck (called "Mose") and sets out for the West alone. The remainder of part one follows Harold in a variety of jobs, from cattle driver to sheepherder, as, always moving further westward, he is adopting the appropriate dress and manners. However, he loses his temper for the second time when he gets into a fight with some intoxicated cattlemen, again shoots one in self-defense, and is forced to flee to the mountains to avoid further trouble.

The second section occurs four years later in the small town of Marmion, Iowa, where "Black Mose," the legendary name given to him by the newspapers, returns to see Mary Yardwell, a girl with whom he fell in love while in prison; for she visited the prisoners and sang hymns. However, learning that she is engaged to be married, he makes plans to set out again for the Rocky Mountains: "He sat with meditative head against the windowpane, listless as a caged and sullen eagle, but his soul was far ahead, swooping above the swells that cut into the murky sky. His eyes studied every rod of soil as he retraced his way up that great wind-swept slope, noting every change in vegetation or settlement. Five years before he had crept like a lizard; now he was rushing straight on like the horning eagle who sees his home crag gleam in the setting sun."[6] Leaving Marmion, he travels through the Grand Canyon, New Mexico, California, and several Indian reservations. During his traveling, he worked at different jobs, including a stint as deputy marshall.

In section three, Black Mose is located three years later in the famous mining camp of Wagon Wheel. There he learns that his mother has died, that his father is coming west, and that Mary, who has broken off her engagement, wants to see him. Out of money, he finally earns enough in a rodeo to return to Chicago to see Mary. While in Chicago he is unable to find a job, becomes very ill, but is nursed back to health by Mary and other friends. Unable to live in the East because he has had a taste of the "high country," he marries Mary and accepts an appointment as an Indian agent at Sand Lake.

While this brief summary may perhaps be too simplistic, it does trace the major movements of the novel. It is not the plot, however, but the portrait of the hero which is the most compelling aspect of the novel. Unfortunately, while Harold's character may be compelling, it is also made to seem unbelievable. Like Garland himself and like Rose Dutcher, who became absorbed with the image of circus-performer William DeLisle, Harold, even at an early age, became absorbed with an image of the West. When he was young his great ambition was to acquire a gun and a horse, "for all the adventurous spirits of the dime novels he had known carried revolvers and rode mustangs. He did not read much, but when he did it was always some tale of fighting."[7] But his greatest ambition was to strike out for the West: "Almost without definable reason the 'Wild West' came to be a land of wonder, lit as by some magical light. Its cañons, *arroyos,* and mesquite, its bronchos, cowboys, Indians, and scouts filled the boy's mind with thoughts of daring, not much unlike the fancies of a boy in the days of knight errantry."[8]

While we know a great deal about Harold's aspirations, we never really know him as a person. At times he becomes little more than the typical Western hero of the dime novels which he reads. The tension between his base instincts and his high aspirations is never developed with the sophistication we find in *Rose of Dutcher's Coolly.* In fact, except for the two episodes in which Harold loses his temper, Garland makes it clear that his emotions are always held in check by a noble sentiment and by a higher purpose. We hear about but never see his involvement in a variety of noble social causes, including the reservation treatment of the Indians.

Harold finally emerges as the romantic individualist; strong, handsome, and self-reliant, he belongs to the class of romantic noblemen who are in quest, not of the Holy Grail, but of the "mystic mountains of the West."[9] Since Black Mose is constantly associated with medieval images of knighthood and chivalry, he suggests that he is a creature from another era. But Garland meant

his character to be taken seriously, and he makes it clear that
Harold will succeed in making a reality of his dream. His aspirations, which are insatiable, will never fully be realized, of course,
so his search will always continue. Just as continual movement
dominates the novel, we suspect that Harold will always be lighting
out for the territory ahead, for "His was the eagle's heart; wild
reaches allured him. Minute beauties of garden or flower were not
for him. The groves along the river had long since lost their charm
because he knew their limits—they no longer appealed to his imagination."[10]

In addition to chivalric images, Harold is also associated with
animal images. On the one hand these images, which suggest his
more base instincts, act as a counterpart to his higher aspirations
represented by the chivalric images. But they also indicate his
closeness to nature; and, when associated with the eagle, they
represent his freedom to stand alone and soar to heights un-
reachable by the common man.

In all of Garland's romantic novels, the bond is no longer the
community, but the one hero. While Garland attempted to create a
new section of the country, with its own unique types of characters,
he did not succeed as well as he had in his middle-border fiction.
The minor characters remain fairly wooden, and the heroes seldom
emerge as much more than types. The travels of his characters often
provide Garland with an opportunity to render magnificent descriptions of the "high country," but, with the exception of his Indian
material, the themes are not compelling enough nor are the
characters sufficiently enough developed to hold our interest.

III   *Two Minor Western Works*

In April, 1899, Garland set sail for England. While he was there
he had the opportunity to meet Sir James Barrie, Bernard Shaw,
Bret Harte, and Thomas Hardy. While Garland was later to discuss
his London excursion in *Roadside Meetings,* a more accurate
recollection of his reactions to London can be found in *Her Mountain Lover* (1901), for which he took copious notes. But, in many
ways, *Her Mountain Lover* continues *The Eagle's Heart* by
providing a similar hero in a different setting. Jim Matteson, the
central character, knows "Black Mose" and tells Englishmen of his
exploits; but he never actually appears in the novel. In fact,
although the novel may properly be treated along with Garland's

other mountain novels, only the final scenes are situated in the Mountain West.

The novel begins in Chicago where Jim, a miner, was called by his partner, Dr. Ramsdell. Because new investments are necessary for their mine, Jim is forced to go to London to find a new partner. He brings back no contract, but a vein is struck that brings wealth to the two partners. Jim also intends to marry Bessie, Dr. Ramsdell's niece.

This novel represents for Garland a double escape—its style as well as its framework are different.In this novel, which he later called his "humorous extravaganza," Garland not only attempts to delve into humor but—as Robert Mane suggests—offers us the incongruous juxtaposition of a typical Western hero in a framework which is in opposition to him. Like Mark Twain's *Innocents Abroad*, we find the likable, dull-witted American with good sense and solid virtues pitted against a degenerating British aristocracy.[11] However, unlike *Innocents Abroad*, Garland's humor usually fails; for Jim is not a buffoon but a perfect Westerner who fails to appear quite real. Even his observers in the novel notice this:

> He was not a clod. He lacked polish and training, but not discernment. Mary's mounting interest in him moved him powerfully, but instead of growing voluble he became silent, and at last looked at her with a meditative, absent-minded stare which puzzled her.
> "It's a strange thing—I can't quite think you are real," she said. "I feel as though I were reading a story."[12]

But Garland proceeds to emphasize that Jim is real and a good deal better than his English counterparts. Even Mary later says, "You make me feel the fascination of the world where clothes count for nothing and where 'society' has no meaning. . . . Oh, I'm heart-weary of the life we call civilized. We're all rotten and dying of it. Nine-tenths of us are degenerates."[13]

But, while Garland's hero is able to pursuade several Englishmen that the "high country" possesses the grandeur which England lacks, the hero, himself, like Harold in *The Eagle's Heart* remains unconvincing. Jean Holloway may be correct when she suggests that "Garland's continued fondness for his quite impossible yarn of a mountain miner in search of British capital leads one to suspect that the 'hustler' was the mouthpiece for certain private impressions of the author which international amity and the pose of cosmopolitan author suppressed elsewhere."[14]

William Dean Howells felt that Garland's group of short stories
collected under the title *They of the High Trails* responded better
to his romantic writings than did *Her Mountain Lover;* Howells
argued in his preface to the collection that Garland's shift of locale
had merely broadened his canvas without weakening his tech-
niques. Nonetheless, this collection, which was not published until
1916, contained several of the stories that had seen prior
publication.[15] In the retitling of the stories, Garland attempted to
delineate the various Western types to be found: "The Grub-
Staker," "The Cow-boss," "The Remittance Man," "The
Lonesome Man," "The Trail Tramp," "The Prospector," "The
Outlaw," "The Leaser," "The Ranger," and "The Tourist."

In an Author's Foreword, Garland undertakes to record all of the
picturesque types found in the West which form the basis of the
collection:

Many changes have swept over the mountain West since twenty years
ago, but romance still clings to the high country. The Grub-Staker, hammer
in hand, still pecking at the float, wanders the hills with hopeful patience,
walking the perilous ledges of the cliffs in endless search of gold.

The Cow-Boss, reckless rear-guard of his kind, still urges his watch-eyed
bronco across the roaring streams, or holds his milling herd in the high
parks, but the Remittance Man, wayward son from across the seas, is gone.
Roused to manhood by his country's call, he has joined the ranks of those
who fight to save the shores of his ancestral isle.

The Prospector still pushes his small pack-mule through the snow of
glacial passes, seeking the unexplored, and therefore more alluring, mountain ranges.

The Lonesome Man still seeks forgetfulness of crime in the solitude,
building his cabin in the shadow of great peaks.

The Trail-Tramp, mounted wanderer, horseman of the restless heart, still
rides from place to place, contemptuous of gold, carrying in his folded
blanket all the vanishing traditions of the wild.

The Fugitive still seeks sanctuary in the green timber—finding the
storms of the granite peaks less to be feared than the fury of the law.

The Leaser—the tenderfoot hay-roller from the prairies—still tries his
luck in some abondoned tunnel, sternly toiling for his faithful sweetheart in
the low country; and

The Forest Ranger, hardy son of the pioneers, representing the finer
social order of the future, rides his lonely woodland trail, guarding with
single-hearted devotion our splendid communal heritage of mine and
stream.[16]

Using lines from the foreword at the beginning of each tale, Garland creates his type. Unfortunately, while the stories often capture the idiosyncrasies of his mountain characters, his characters are usually picturesque, and the scenes are often compelling, the characters again seldom emerge from their type. As Jean Holloway suggests, what was lacking was the emotional identification with his subject matter which had given *Main-Travelled Roads* its vital impact. In the Mountain West, Garland remained a sympathetic observer, but an outsider nevertheless.[17]

All of the stories in *They of the High Trails* are dominated by a single attitude—a belief in individual freedom and in the abundant possibilities of the West. The deprivation found in Garland's middle-border fiction is absent. In the opening story, "The Grub-Staker," Sherm Bidwell, who has spent twenty years unsuccessfully prospecting for gold, finally strikes a vein. With Widow Maggie Delaney, he begins hiding his fortune; but, since news of his success is soon known, everyone begins rushing to the mine and staking claims. Refusing several offers by large companies for their claim, Sherm and Maggie are married at a ceremony at the mine; and the story ends with the "newlywed's" anticipation of their prosperous life. Despite the fact that there is minimal character development or tension in the story, the local color, especially the gold fever, is effectively captured. Also, in the best tradition of Bret Harte, a heart-warming simplicity is found in the characters, and a sympathetic treatment is given the lovers who are not young, but who are nevertheless optimistic.

A similar treatment of love is found in "The Leaser" where again the lovers are not young. Although, as in all of these stories, the hint of tragedy is missing, the lovers evoke our sympathy. The hero fled the farm eleven years earlier on an impulse. After several adventures, he takes a lease on a concession and is now well supplied with money. Returning to the country, he equips himself with an automobile and other necessities and visits his former fiancée. Although she is older, she is still pretty; and the couple decide to marry. The possibility of happiness recalls the ending of "A Branch Road," although the misery of Agnes' present life in "A Branch Road" is not suggested, much less described.

Although most of the stories in the collection end on a note of love, the lovers are usually younger. In "The Cow-Boss," Roy Pierce, a cattle farmer, dislikes the postmaster and decides to "rough him up." However, before the encounter, Lida, the post-master's niece, informs the cowboys that he is sick. Eventually, Roy falls in love with her, but she rejects him when she learns what he had intended to do. In the end, however, she forgives him. While there is not much conflict in the story, there is some good local humor; and Roy emerges as an effective type, one similar to some of Garland's farm characters in *Prairie Folks*.

Not only is the deprivation found in *Main-Travelled Roads* lacking in *They of the High Trails*, but money and opportunity are available, either through hard work or through marriage. In "The Remittance Man" Lester, the "remittance man," was a youth sent to American by his parents on the pretense of his learning to raise cattle, but in reality to get him out of their life. He goes to stay at Blondell's Ranch where he and Fan Blondell fall in love. Although he feels superior to the other ranch hands and is lazy, they marry, despite the objections of her parents. After their marriage, he is confronted by some ruffians and is hurt when he is thrown from his horse. After he recovers, he resolves to work hard and not feel superior.

As in "The Remittance Man," the luck of the hero in "The Ranger" follows the same path: he marries a girl who is living with an old man in a valley. When villainous scoundrels attack her, even accuse her of a crime, the ranger helps her—and conquers her, only to learn that she is a millionaire's daughter. A more fascinating story, and one which seems out of place in this collection, is "The Lonesome Man." While it is told against the backdrop of a love story, we do not learn about this background until the end. Since the story relates how a wandering stranger apparently happens upon a lonesome miner, the miner spends the better part of the story talking about his loneliness; his lack of human contact seems unbearable. When the stranger and the miner discuss what made him become a hermit, the miner reveals that he was in love with a woman who, he discovered, was having an affair with another man. He fled after killing them both. When the miner then asked who the stranger was, he replied:

"I am the avenger . . . the man you hated was my brother. The woman you killed was his wife."

The fugitive fell upon his knees with a cry like that of one being strangled. Out of the darkness a red flame darted, and the crouching man fell to the floor, a crumpled, bloody heap.

For a long time the executioner stood above the body, waiting, listening from the shadow to the faint receding breath-strokes of his victim. When it was still he restored his weapon to its sheath and stepped over the threshold into the keen and pleasant night.

As he closed the door behind him the stranger raised his eyes to Solidor, whose sovereign, cloud-like crest swayed among the stars.

"Now I shall rest," he said, with solemn satisfaction.[18]

The surprise, violent ending was different for Garland; and the method of handling the isolation gives the story a Hawthornian or Poesque quality.

Of all the characters in *They of the High Trails*, only Ed Kelley is developed beyond a mere framework. The hero of three separate stories under the title "The Trail Tramp" ("Kelley Afoot," "Kelley as Marshall," and "Partners for a Day"), Kelley is always on the move, working at whatever job is available. In many ways Kelley resembles a mature Harold Excell: in each of the three places Kelley goes, he attempts to do something good; but he refuses to make lasting commitments, since he is by nature a saddle tramp. Kelley appears throughout Garland's romantic writings, but Garland, who wanted to create a novel around him, or assemble a series of stories around him, never succeeded. Even in *Hesper*, Kelley remains a secondary character.

They of the High Trails remains a pleasant but undistinguished collection. Garland's fiction seemed to gain strength when he became emotionally attached to his subject matter, and such was not the case in *They of the High Trails*. Such was the case, however, with the American Indian.

IV   *The World of the American Indian*

By the beginning of the nineteenth century the ubiquitous "captivity narrative" was a standard source for thrilling details of frontier life. As Roy Harvey Pearce suggests in *The Savages of America*, the Indian of the captivity narrative was the consummate villain—a beast who smashed the skulls of infants and carried off the women. This was the price, according to the narratives, that a peace-loving farmer, a proponent of civilization, paid for attempting to live in the presence of bloody savages. These narratives were frenetic attempts to hold on to the crudest image of the triumphantly brutal Indian.

The accounts of Indian atrocities excited the imagination of readers, particularly those unfamiliar with frontier life.

But, in fact, readers also saw a discrepancy between what they read and what they experienced, for they knew that the Indian was not destined to triumph gloriously. When they saw Indians, they were dispossessed, degraded, and diseased; and the readers knew that the Indians beyond the frontier would eventually be in no better condition.[19] Whatever excitement was stirred in the imagination of the reader, it was clear that the Indians would be destroyed; for, despite the intellectual inquiry into the nature of primitivism and into the moral worth of an individual Indian, the way of life of the Indian and his culture were not only alien to the white man, but they appeared to impede progress and to pose a threat to civilization. But, although the scenes of horror and portrayals of the Indian which were detailed in the captivity narratives usually did not fit the facts, and although readers saw a different Indian because of their limited experiences, the literary accounts nevertheless helped substantiate the theory that the Indian must be destroyed for the good of civilization.

While wholesale slaughter occurred in many instances, it was considered to be more convenient and virtuous to convert the Indian to white ways whenever possible. The missionaries desperately attempted to Christianize the Indian, and, by extension, to civilize him, since the two effects were equated in the minds of most white Americans. Usually civilizing efforts were directed at attempting to teach the Indian how to farm the land, for agriculture was considered a mark of civilization which would raise the Indian out of his savage past and bring him into the mainstream of American civilization. The efforts of the missionaries were such failures that few missionaries continued to feel that such a conversion could be effected; but, since most of them had little understanding of Indian culture, their failures were largely a result of this misunderstanding. One missionary, James Knowles, concluded in 1834 that it was a divine plan that the Indians be destroyed because they could not obey the "great law of God which obliged them to be civilized, and to adopt those modes of life which would enable their territory to support the greatest number of inhabitants." Americans, he continued, could fulfill their destiny "by saving from ruin the helpless descendants of the savage."[20]

The ambivalence toward the Indian continued throughout most of the literature of the nineteenth century, but his fate was neverthless assured. Between 1860 and 1890 the Indian was virtually dispossessed; his culture and his civilization as he had known them were destroyed. The Wounded Knee massacre in 1890 signaled the symbolic end of Indian freedom, for by 1890 the frontier had officially been declared closed; Geronimo, the last of the great Apache chiefs, had surrendered; Sitting Bull, a great Sioux leader, was killed; and the Ghost Dance, a ritual performed to bring back the lost Indian past, failed. The removal of the Indian was merely the beginning of his loss of freedom which was inevitable given the context of the Puritan myth and the nineteenth-century belief in Manifest Destiny.

In the twentieth century the treatment in literature of the American Indian generally falls into three categories: (1) the negative stereotype of the ignoble savage but which also includes acknowledgments of strength and individual nobility; (2) treatment of the Indian as a simple creature of an inferior culture which is passing; and (3) a sympathetic response to the mistreated Indian with a recognition of his unique culture.[21] By far the strongest trend in recent literature is a sympathetic response to the Indian, a sympathy imbued with a growing understanding of his culture. Not only does the literature betray guilt concerning both the extermination of the Indian and his way of life, as well as guilt concerning the reservation treatment of the surviving Indians, but there is an attempt to portray the Indian as a human being in all his complexity and to portray the human elements of his conflict with the dominant culture.

Hamlin Garland was one of the first writers in the twentieth century to depart from traditional ways of portraying the Indian. Unlike James Fenimore Cooper before him who had little personal contact with Indians but who drew upon what he considered the most authentic sources for his material, particularly John Heckewelder's *History, Manners, and Customs of the Indian Nations* (1819) and Nicholas Biddle's *History of the Expedition Under the Command of Lewis and Clark* (1814),[22] Garland had the opportunity to live with the Indians for a time. Consequently, he reacted strongly against those writers who treated the Indians as nothing more than savage beasts. As he told Major Stouch, the Indian agent at Darlington, Oklahoma, "We have had plenty of the 'wily redskin' kind of thing. . . . I am going to tell of the red man as you and Seger have known him, as a man of the polished stone age trying to adapt himself to steam and electricity."[23]

Garland became indignant over the unjust treatment of the Indian. He was not concerned with the forces which subjugated the Indian as much as he was with the conflicts which arose when the Indian attempted to come to terms with an alien culture. He had little patience with white programs which attempted to rehabilitate a defeated race and had little understanding of the Indian's way of life. However, he also appreciated the inherent tragedy and futility in the attempt of many Indians to retain their way of life in modern society. But Garland ultimately makes it clear that the Indian must change. His primary concern, as James K. Folsom has observed, is with the nature of the process of conversion.[24]

In Garland's stories collected in *The Book of the American Indian* (1923), which also contains the epic "The Silent Eaters"—a fictionalized biography of Sitting Bull—he manifests an engaging and genuine sympathy for the American Indian. In his best stories, his treatment has an authenticity unmatched in his other writings during this period; and the theme of the necessity of conversion to modern life, throughout the collection, is most effectively treated in "Wahiah—A Spartan Mother." Garland first says of the Cheyenne and Arapahoe village that "to the careless observer this village was lonely, repulsive; to the sympathetic mind it was a place of drama, for there the passions, prejudices, ancestral loves and hates of the two races met and clashed. There the man of the polished stone age was trying, piteously, tragically, trying, to take on the manner of life of a race ten thousand years in advance of him, and there a few devoted Quakers were attempting to lead the nomads into the ways of the people of the plow."[25]

Here John Seger, the Indian agent among the Cheyennes and Arapahoes, tries to convince the Indians to send their children to school. Most comply, but Tomacham and his wife, Wahiah, resist sending their son, Atokan, since it would mean that he would be forced to change his dress and to follow the white man's road. They eventually agree, recognizing that "we are on the road—we cannot turn back."[26] When Seger resolves to whip the offenders, because of flagrant truancy, many parents are unhappy; they feel that "It was pivotal, this question of punishment—it marked their final subjection to the white man."[27] When Atokan is truant, Seger, whips him in front of his parents and others until the boy's spirit is broken. Seger justifies his actions to Atokan's parents by telling them that the children must learn to plow and reap as the white man does or they will die. After the whipping, the parents surrender; and, in a symbolic gesture, Wahiah breaks her son's "symbols of freedom," his bows and arrows, and orders him henceforth to obey the agent. The story is central in the collection, for it effectively dramatizes the painful realization by Wahiah of the necessity to reject the old ways.

This theme is also treated in "Nistina" and "The New Medicine House," but it is handled more directly in "Rising Wolf-Ghost Dancer." Rising Wolf recounts how in his young life he became a medicine man. After the Indian defeat, Rising Wolf and his people are placed on reservations where his powers are no longer needed. However, their hopes are raised when a stranger teaches them the Ghost Dance, which promises to bring back their lost past. If they arrange to dance for four days, the white man would presumably disappear on the fourth day, the buffalo would return, and the Indians would be reunited with their dead on earth. The dance is performed, but is unsuccessful, since the whites are still there. Convinced that the Ghost Dance and the Indian medicine have both been in error, Rising Wolf renounces them and resolves to take up white ways:

I had made up my mind. The white man's trail was wide and dusty by reason of many feet passing thereon, but it was long. The trail of my people was ended.

I said "I will follow the white man's trail. I will make him my friend, but I will not bend my neck to his burdens. I will be cunning as the coyote. I will ask him to help me to understand his ways, and then I will prepare the way for my own children. Maybe they will outrun the white man in his own shoes. Anyhow, there are but two ways. One leads to hunger and death, the other leads where the poor white man lives. Beyond is the happy hunting ground, where the white man cannot go."[28]

To be sure, not all Indians are converted. In "Big Moggasen," the chief of a Navajo band, living high in the mountains, refuses to have anything to do with the white man and rejects any help for his desolate tribe. Finally, persuaded to visit Little Father, he is offered aid in return for sending his children away to be schooled by whites. He refuses and leaves, for he has resolved to resist the new road.

Generally, Garland's heroes are either Indian agents or schoolteachers who show a tolerance and sympathetic understanding toward the Indian. The villains tend to be missionaries who attempt to convert the Indian not by teaching him new ways but by eradicating all of his customs. In one of his most poignant stories,

"The Iron Kiva," Garland tells of two children who escape and kill themselves rather than be taken away to school in the East by a missionary. The Indian's attitude toward the missionaries is directly stated: "They came to love one of those who taught them—a white woman with a gentle face—but the man in the black coat who told the children that the religion of their father's was wicked and foolish—him they hated and bitterly despised."[29] Garland thus indicated that, to convert the Indian, it is not necessary to entirely destroy his customs but to teach him the skills necessary to endure in a dominant white society.

Not all of the stories treat the theme of conversion, for some deal strictly with Indian customs. In "The Remorse of Waumdisapa," we find dissention in the camp of Waumdisapa, chief of the Tetons. Matawan, his cousin, jealous of the chief's great fame, was conspiring to degrade and destroy him. At a council meeting, Waumdisapa announces that he would step aside if his doing so were the will of the members. But when each spoke in his defense and Matawan accused the group of cowardice, Waumdisapa, losing control, leaped up and stabbed him to death. Full of remorse for the murder, he removed himself as chief and took his place outside the council circle—self-accused and self-deposed.

In "The Decree of Council," Garland indicates that the white man's road cannot nor should not always be followed. In this story, Big Nose, an inveterate gambler, foolishly gambles away both his wives and his belongings. After consideration the council decreed to give him back one of his wives—the older one who was difficult to manage. Unhappy with the decision, he nevertheless endured for several years, gave up gambling, worked hard, and became one of the most progressive men in the camp. However, no longer able to endure his wife, and wanting to take a new one, he approached Seger, the superintendent of the school, to get advice, feeling that since he was walking the white man's road, he did not care what the other Indians had to say. But Seger, recognizing the cultural differences, accepts the judgment of White Shield that, from the decree of the council, there is no appeal.

The most powerful story in the collection, "The Story of Howling Wolf," is also the most somber because it seriously questions the positive view expressed elsewhere of the potential for conversion by following the white man's road. Seven years after Howling Wolf's brother was shot by two white cattlemen, Howling Wolf vows to kill the men responsible. Captain Cook attempts to gain his trust; but, to Howling Wolf, "It was hard to trust the white man even when he smiled, for his tongue had ever been forked like a rattlesnake and his hand exceedingly cunning. . . . They brought plows that tore the sod, machines that swept away the grass. They all said, 'Dam Injun,' and in those words displayed their hearts."[30]

But Howling Wolf finally decides to trust Cook with whom he makes friends, renounces his vengeance, resolves to win the respect of whites, and writes his resolution on a piece of paper. He gets a job hauling hides; but the whites continue to taunt him. When a cowboy picks a fight with him and fires a wild shot, wounding another white man in the knee, Howling Wolf is blamed. To avoid being lynched, he is jailed; and the agent's efforts to get him released are futile. One day Howling Wolf is taken from the jail by the sheriff, who wants to attend a baseball game, but is afraid to leave him unattended. Howling Wolf, however, thinks he is being taken to his execution and tries to escape. He is pursued by a mob and caught after being abandoned by the sheriff, and the mob "With the light of hell on their faces . . . shot down the defenseless man and then alighted, and, with remorseless hate, crushed his face beneath their feet as if he were a rattlesnake. They stabbed his dead body and shot it full of bullets. They fought for a chance to kick him. They lost all resemblance to men. Wolves fighting over the flesh of their own kind could not have been more heartlessly malevolent—more appalling in their ferocity."[31] Although the Indian finally recovers, his is so misshappen and battered that even his wife could not recognize him.

Howling Wolf's attempt to walk the white man's road ends tragically. As James Folsom observes, Howling Wolf's story, like others in the volume, is a treatment of education; but what he learns stands in direct opposition to the lesson learned elsewhere; for, except for the actions of the agent, his education teaches the cruelty, savagery, and selfishness of the whites. Their evil is not a product of different social values which could be corrected through social action but an expression of the bestiality in man. The lesson here is that, while change may be inevitable, it does not necessarily represent progress.[32]

Garland combines the theme of the necessity of change with an indignation over the reservation treatment of the Indian most effectively in "The Silent Eaters." In this fictionalized biography of Sitting Bull, Garland traces the history of the Sioux nation from its long self-sufficiency to the eventual subjugation and decline of the

race that culminates with the death of Sitting Bull. Garland's choice
of a narrator provides him with the opportunity not only to portray
Sitting Bull sympathetically but, through the narrator's development, to indicate the necessity of change if the Indian is to survive.
The story is told by Iapi, the son of Shato and a member of "The
Silent Eaters," a band of trusted warriors used by the chief primarily as advisors. These warriors were called "The Silent Eaters"
because "they met in private feasts and talked quietly without songs
or dancing, whereas all the others in the tribe danced and made
merry. With these 'Silent Eaters' the chief freely discussed all the
great problems which arose."[33]

When Sitting Bull surrenders, Iapi is befriended by Lieutenant
Davis, who gives him the opportunity to learn the white man's ways
by sending him to the East to study. Almost a spokesman for
Darwinian evolution, Davis, who has tremendous respect for the
Sioux, also convinces Iapi that he will need to advance his education
if he wishes to keep his people. As Iapi says, "He [Davis] was a
philosopher. He had no hate of any race. He looked upon each people as the product of its conditions, and he often said, 'the plains Indian was a perfect adaptation of organism to environment till the
whites disturbed him.' "[34] Although Iapi sympathizes with Sitting
Bull, he also senses the futility of attempting to maintain a way of
life when the environment is no longer suitable.

Upon Iapi's return from the East, he gives a realistic account of
the conditions on the reservation: "They were like poor white
farmers, ragged, dirty, and bent. The clothes they wore were shod-
dy grey and deeply repulsive to me. Their robes of buffalo, their
leggins of buckskin, their beaded pouches—all the things I
remembered with pride—had been worn out (or sold). Even the
proud warriors of my tribe were reduced to the condition of those
who are at once prisoners and beggars."[35] As in "Rising Wolf-Ghost
Dance," the Indians, in a sensitive scene, futilely perform the Ghost
Dance, hoping to recapture a lost past. When the dance is unsuccessful, Sitting Bull and "The Silent Eaters" are killed by Indian
traitors. The tragic history of Sitting Bull is viewed by Iapi in epic
terms, for Sitting Bull becomes a metaphor for the Sioux Nation:

He epitomized the epic, tragic story of my kind. His life spanned the gulf
between the days of our freedom and the death of every custom native to
us. He saw the invader come and he watched the buffalo disappear. Within
the half century of his conscious life span he witnessed greater changes and

comprehended more of my tribe's tragic history than any other red man. . . . He will grow bigger like a mountain as he recedes into the past. He was chief among red men and we shall never see his like again. If the Great Spirit does not hate his red children, our Father is happy in the home of the spirits—the land of the returning buffalo.[36]

Slightly less successful artistically than the stories which comprise *The Book of the American Indian*, although more successful commercially (selling nearly 100,000 copies), was Garland's ambitious study of Indian problems in his novel *The Captain of the Gray-Horse Troop* (1902). Generally well received by reviewers, it was also highly praised by President Theodore Roosevelt, who attempted to implement some of Garland's suggestions incorporated in the novel.

The novel was partially based on an outbreak of the Northern Cheyennes which was instigated by the actions of cattlemen. The story, situated at Fort Smith near Pinion City, Montana, reflects with vivid accuracy the reservation life and the problems of the Teton Sioux. Captain George Curtis is detached on a special assignment to supplant the corrupt Indian agent, Sennett. Arriving at the post with his sister, Jennie, he finds tensions mounting between the Indians and the cattlemen who are determined to drive the Indians from their lands. The cattlemen's cause is aided by the powerful Senator Brisbane, whose attitude toward the Indians reflects those of the cattlemen: " 'Human beings!' sneered Brisbane 'they are nothing but a greasy lot of vermin—worthless from every point of view. Their rights can't stand in the way of civilization.' "[37]

Curtis' situation is additionally complicated when he falls in love with Brisbane's niece, Elsie, and must convert her to his sympathetic point of view, one in which the Indian is regarded as a human being with individual rights. Moreover, Curtis must find a way in which to prevent an outbreak and, at the same time, help the Indians progress. The situation intensifies through a series of violent scenes that culminate in the death of a sheepherder and in the delivery of the responsible Indian by Curtis into the hands of justice at Pinion City. Because precautionary measures by the agent to protect the Indian are unsatisfactory, the prisoner is shot and dragged to death by a mob. This outrage, however, produces a reaction: Senator Brisbane is defeated; the settlers withdraw from the reservation; and the federal government, which was previously applying pressure on Curtis, passes a purchase bill to protect the Indians and their land. Curtis and Elsie marry, and they begin helping the Indians change from a hunting to a farming community.

Like many of the stories in *The Book of the American Indian*, Garland stresses in his novel the necessity of conversion for the Indians; but he also urges the cooperation of sympathetic whites in this process. As in *The Eagle's Heart*, the cattlemen are the villains, since their goals and greed make this cooperation difficult. As for the good aspects about *The Captain of the Gray-Horse Troop*, the plot is related to the principal themes effectively, and the descriptions of the reservation life of the Indians are evocative. However, the novel suffers from the weaknesses in characterization. The character of Captain Curtis, while clearly sympathetic, does not emerge much more than did that of Harold Excell; rather, he serves primarily as a mouthpiece for Garland and as a vehicle for Garland's views on reform. But, generally, his treatment of the American Indian in the novel, as well as in *The Book of the American Indian*, illustrates not only Garland's social concerns during this period, but also some of the best writing that he ever accomplished.

V   *The World of the Miner*

Between 1903 and 1907 Garland published three novels—*Hesper* (1903), *Witch's Gold* (1906), and *Money Magic* (1907)—in which the scene shifts from the world of the mountaineer to that of the miner. Although less successful than his Indian material, these novels offer a continuation of the earlier mountain novels and complete Garland's picture of Western life. But, unlike the treatment of females in his other mountain novels, in each of those works Garland shifts the main subject back to a woman.

Of these novels, *Hesper* is probably the most interesting. In a handwritten preface to the novel, dated "West Salem, 1903," Garland discussed the background for the novel:

That *Hesper* is my most romantic novel I must admit, and yet like all my other stories of the mountains, it is based on a careful study of the scenes and issues involved.

The stage for the story was already prepared. For ten years I had been absorbing Colorado life and scenery and the region roundabout Cripple Creek was vividly mapped in my mind. The Bull Hill Miner's War had but lately taken place and I was not only familiar with the conditions which had led to this exciting contest, but I knew some of the chief actors in it.

Precisely as the Cheyenne outbreak of 1897 had served me as a sociologic background for *The Captain of the Gray-Horse Troop*, so the Miner's War in Cripple Creek now offered a picturesque and dramatic episode in Western history to my pen.[38]

The story begins in New York where Louis Rupert and his sister Ann prepare to leave for the Rockies. On their first night in Colorado Springs, while staying on a ranch owned by their cousins, the Barnetts, they observe a fight in which a cowboy wounds Rob Raymond, the foreman. Attending Rob at his bedside while he recuperates, Ann quickly falls in love with him. But, realizing the obstacles involved, Rob leaves to join the gold seekers around Cripple Creek where he meets and forms a partnership with Matt Kelly which results in their fortune. But, when a miner's strike occurs, Jack Munro, a friend of Rob's from West Point, arrives to help organize the miners; and he becomes a rival for Ann's love, as does Peabody, her former lover from New York who has come to take Ann back with him.

During the strike, Rob becomes a hero. Since Rob refuses to side with either party, both sides perceive him as an enemy. His mine is dynamited because—as Rob thinks—he refused to side with the miners. But he becomes a peacemaker, first by warning the miners of a planned secret arrival of the sheriff, and then by kidnapping Munro to avoid a confrontation between the miners and the military. Munro returns too late, but is still killed in a scuffle. Ann, who had returned to New York, telegraphs Rob, asking him to bring her back to the Rockies where they will make their home.

Although the setting of the novel is the miner's strike, the story is disappointing from both historical and sociological points of view. The reader gains only a superficial understanding of the causes of the conflict between the free miners, the union men, and the mine owners. And, unlike Garland's treatment of the poor city workers in the first part of *Jason Edwards* or of the depressing farm conditions in many of his short stories, the depressed economic condition of the miners is scarcely touched upon. Furthermore, since we are never shown the miners at work, we are prevented from appreciating their struggles, despite the fact that Garland's sympathies clearly lie with the free miners.

But, while the lack of details in the social background hurts the novel, the mining camp is not really its subject. Rather, Garland is more concerned with the transformation of Ann Rupert from an

Easterner to a Westerner. Like the Hesperides in Greek mythology, the "daughters of the evening" who dwelt in a garden on the Far West in which there were apples of gold, Ann changes her name to Hesper, the name originally desired by her father, and thereby completes her transformation. Unfortunately, while Ann is the proper subject of the novel, her transformation seems too mechanical. Her character is so inadequately developed because Garland seems more interested in the demands of his romantic plot. In fact, none of the other characters, with the possible exception of Matt Kelly, emerges far beyond Western prototypes.

As in his other romantic works, Garland's mountain setting is described so powerfully that the characters seem dwarfed by it. In a fashion that is reminiscent of the final scenes of Norris' *The Octopus*, Garland depicts the insignificance of man's struggle amid the power and magnificence of nature:

And over all—over Raymond and Kelly, dusty and bleeding, working with their men to rescue the imprisoned miners deep below—over the swarming groups of shivering women on the hill, over the bitter and savage ranks of the Vendettes, over the whole great, silent range, the sunlight poured in splendor—warm and golden as October—and a soft wind from the west brought rose-tinted clouds sailing like gentle doves of peace from the far-off Crestones, impassive and serene. "What is it all about, my little men?" Mogalyon seemed to ask, concerned as he was with the affairs of geologic cycles and the return of waters to the sea.[39]

In Garland's second "miners" novel, *Witch's Gold*, which was first published as *The Spirit of Sweetwater* in 1898, he gives us a conventional love story with little complication. Clement, an owner of a rich mine, has come to Colorado Springs to find a wife. When he discovers Ellice Ross, who is nearly dead, he takes her in and cares for her; and, under his influence, she regains the will to live. Here again, Garland is less concerned with the social background of the novel than with the noble sentiments of the characters and the mystical qualities of the mountains. Indeed, Ellice has to go to Pike's Peak in order to regain fully her health.

Colorado Springs again provided the setting for Garland's next novel, *Money Magic* (1907). Garland discussed the origins of the story which he first titled "Mart Haney's Mate": "The chief characters of this novel were suggested to me by a young girl, the manager of a hotel in a little Colorado town, and her lover, a big Irish gambler I once observed in Cripple Creek. I had no talk with the girl, but as I watched her in her defensive warfare against the cattlemen, drummers, and miners who frequented the hotel, I wondered what would happen if Mart Haney of Cripple Creek should happen to lunch at the Golden Eagle Hotel."[40]

Here Garland combines the theme of the lure and power of money with the maturation of a young girl who is torn between desire and duty, rather than between the East and the West. An old miner, Mart Haney, rich from gambling, desires to marry a young girl but is rejected. To convince her of his sincerity, he abandons his casino. Ironically, an unlucky gambler, who does not know that Haney no longer works at the casino, provokes a gunfight and wounds Haney. Bertha, the young woman, is brought to him quickly so he can marry her and leave her his fortune before he dies. He survives, however, and Bertha remains at his bedside, his devoted wife. Although she eventually falls in love with Ben Fordyce, a young lawyer, she is so drawn to her husband out of duty that she will not abandon him. Nobly, Mart chooses to give his wife freedom and money: he goes to the mountains where he knows the altitude will be fatal to his heart.

Although the plot is sentimental, the treatment of Bertha redeems the story. While Bertha is not as fully realized as was Rose of Dutcher's Coolly, the psychological tension is convincing. Suddenly confronted with a good deal of wealth, she feels ennobled by the grace of money, but she cannot find peace by abandoning her husband. Garland effectively captured the lure of money, but, unlike his contemporaries, Howells, Norris, and Dreiser, he did not see this attraction as potentially destructive. Like Rose Dutcher, Bertha, also physically attractive and vivacious, is transformed from an unpolished Western girl into a refined woman.

With the addition of a couple of minor novels dealing with forestry, *Cavanaugh, Forest Ranger* (1910) and *The Forester's Daughter* (1914) and with a revival of his interest in psychic experimentation which was the subject of *Tyranny of the Dark* (1905), *The Shadow World* (1908), and *Victor Olnee's Discipline* (1911), Garland had completed his picture of "the high country" and was prepared to look elsewhere for his material. Garland's mountain fiction clearly contains some of his best writing. His poetic descriptions of nature are rendered with both power and sensitivity. He was able to capture the romance that the West seemed to promise. His heroes and heroines are lured to a land which seemed to hold a mystic promise, and Garland vividly portrayed their excitement, anticipation, and disappointments. Though Garland's mountain fiction often failed, Howells' comment on *Hesper* may well serve as a fair assessment of all of Garland's mountain fiction: "It is a fine book, full of manly poetry and a high ideal."[41]

CHAPTER 7

A Return to the Past

I A Turn to Autobiography

BY 1911, Garland's literary career seemed to be approaching a dead end: critics had been unanimous in disparaging his recent fiction. Physically ill and mentally weary, he futilely attempted to block out new material.[1] As his interest in fiction declined, he began to feel the need to deal more directly and fully with the major events of his own life. If he could not create material out of new experiences, he could re-create the past.

Although Garland's fiction was, from the beginning, never without autobiographical elements, he was determined by 1911 to give his career a new direction by turning to autobiography as his chief literary form. With this intention he undertook *A Son of the Middle Border* in late 1911; and after several revisions, it was published in book-length form in 1917. Encouraged by its almost instantaneous success, which not only brought about his election to the American Academy of Arts and Letters and was a prime factor in his being awarded the Pulitzer Prize in 1922, but also reestablished him as a major literary figure, Garland proceeded to write three more autobiographical volumes: *A Daughter of the Middle Border* (1921), *Trail Makers of the Middle Border* (1926), and *Back-Trailers From the Middle Border* (1928). He also published four volumes of literary reminiscences: *Roadside Meetings* (1930), *Companions on the Trail* (1931), *My Friendly Contemporaries* (1932), and *Afternoon Neighbors* (1934). Thus, through autobiography, Garland had discovered his final literary voice, which he used until his death in 1940.

II Boy Life on the Prairie

Garland's first major autobiographical effort, however, was *Boy Life on the Prairie* (1899), which developed from a series of articles,

"Boy-Life on the Prairie," which he wrote in 1887 and published in the *American Magazine* in 1888.[2] The six articles, which describe a year's cycle of farm activities from the point of view of a boy in the 1870s, begin with cornhusking in late fall and conclude with the melons and early frosts of the following year. The collection is a mixture of informative detail, which includes accounts of the painful realities of Western farm life, and of a nostaligic attempt to dwell on the lost world of Garland's boyhood. As Donald Pizer observes, the articles are best in Garland's ability to evoke the reality of particular moments and moods of boy-life on the farm—both the despair and pain of many unpleasant duties like cornhusking as well as the exhilaration of horseback rides, games, prairie meals, and dances.[3]

While in all of the articles Garland speaks in his own person, addressing Eastern readers and informing them in detail about the realities of Western farm life, only in the last article, "Melons and Early Frosts," does he depart from his boy's point of view and address himself to the changing conditions of farm life and the difficult role of the farmer's wife.

While the six articles form the heart of *Boy Life on the Prairie*, retaining the boy's world and preserving much of the cyclic structure, the much revised and expanded version increases in range and depth by dealing with Garland's boyhood experiences on an Iowa farm from approximately 1869 to 1881. Garland wanted to write *Boy Life* as fiction rather than as an autobiography in the strictest sense. He emphasized this intent in his preface to the 1899 edition of *Boy Life:* "It is not my intention to present in *Lincoln Stewart* the details of my own life and character, though I lived substantially the life of the boys herein depicted. I have used *Lincoln* merely as a connecting life-thread to bind the chapters together. . . . In short, I have aimed to depict boy life, not boys; the characterization is incidental. *Lincoln* and *Rance* and *Milton* and *Owen* are to be taken as types rather than as individuals."[4]

Garland's introduction to the 1926 Allyn and Bacon school edition, however, acknowledged that the book was essentially autobiographical:

My plan, my critics say, was nobler than my product, and with this I must agree; but at its lowest you will find . . . an honest and careful attempt to delineate a border community building and planting from 1870 to 1880—a settlement as seen and shared by a boy from ten to twenty.

You may, if you wish, substitute Richard Garland for "Duncan Stewart," Hamlin for "Lincoln," and Frank for "Owen," for this book is substantially made up of the doings of my own family. . . . all of the events, even those in fictional form, are actual, although in some cases I have combined experiences of other boys with my own.[5]

Still, Garland's intention here is the same as it was in the articles, because he wanted to include characteristic experiences of a typical prairie youth rather than to center on the particular characteristics of his own youth which he did do in *Son of the Middle Border*. Thus, in *Boy Life* he told the story through the third person in order to give the story less of an autobiographical pose.

As Bruce R. McElderry, Jr., has noted, despite the apparent discursiveness of the book, Garland achieved unity by his emphasis upon the change in the prairie, one which parallels the boy's maturation. There is a gradual shift of emphasis which implies the change from boy to man.[6] The action, which is built around the development of the central observer, Lincoln Stewart, begins with his family's arrival in Iowa and ends with his departure for school in town. In the conclusion, Lincoln visits Sun Prairie once again when he is twenty-four years old and reflects on the changes on the prairie—the diminishing wheat fields, the predomiance of the dairy interest, the loss of the wild meadows. But the real change was in Lincoln himself who vainly attempts to recapture his lost boyhood: "Something mystical had gone out of it all. It was not so important as his imagination had made it. It was simpler, thinner of texture someway, and he drove on with a feeling of disappointment."[7]

While there is a sense of general chronological development from the beginning to the end, the narrative effect is achieved by a careful selection of episodes, each of which has a dramatic movement of its own; and, taken together, these depict the full range of pleasant and unpleasant activities and adventures which typify a boy's experiences on a prairie farm, as indicated by a brief glance at some of the chapter titles: "The Fall's Ploughing," "Seeding," "Planting Corn," "Herding the Cattle," "A Fourth of July Celebration," "The Old-Fashioned Threshing," "Threshing in the Field," "The Corn Husking," "The Coming of the Circus," "A Camping Trip," "Owen Rides at the County Fair," "Visiting Schools," "Momentous Wolf-hunt."

Garland is able not only to provide much factual information (as he had done in his series of articles) but, more importantly, to evoke

the pleasures and pains of farm life from a boy's point of view. We
are able to participate in the monotony and difficulty of fall
ploughing, harvesting, and husking corn, as well as in such delightful experiences as haying, planting corn, swimming, riding, and
camping. He makes us see that, taken as a whole, boy life on the
prairie was not a bad experience; and he is especially effective in
evoking the mood of particular moments. Recalling Rose Dutcher,
for example, we can experience with Lincoln the enchantment and
charm of the circus performers as well as the terror that the
rattlesnake brings.

Occasionally, Garland uses these moments not only as self-
contained episodes but also as symbolized stages in Lincoln's
growth. This technique is best illustrated in Lincoln's idealization of
Rance Knapp's skill in riding and hunting. The herd of wild horses
seen at the end of Chapter One symbolizes the freedom of prairie
life. Throughout the narrative constant reference is made to Rance's
horse, Ladrone, which represents not only this freedom but the
boy's youth in general. At the end of the narrative, when Lincoln
returns to the prairie no longer a boy, Garland inserts a poem,
"Ladrone," which reflects the loss of youth:

> And "what of Ladrone"—do you ask?
> Oh! friend, I am sad at the name
>
> . . . .
>
> O magic west wind of the mountains
> O steed with the stinging mane,
> In sleep I draw rein at the fountain,
> And wake with a shiver of pain;
> For the heart and heat of the city
> Are walls and prison and chain.
> Lost my Ladrone—gone the wild living—
> I dream, but my dreaming is vain.[8]

Boy Life is a lively narrative of a pervasive American experience
of growing up on the farm in the nineteenth century. But, as
Donald Pizer observes, the work is essentially a boy's book; its
themes do not extend far beyond a boy's vision or an adult's
nostalgia.[9] While many of the nostalgic recollections are told with
colorful detail and dramatic force, the possibility of tragedy is never
present. In *A Son of the Middle Border,* Garland was able to go
beyond a boy's vision and to interpret the major stages and conflicts
in his own personal development.

III   *Toward* A Son of the Middle Border

After the publication of *Boy Life* in 1899, Garland turned his attention to the Mountain West and only occasionally produced an autobiographical sketch. Toward the end of this period, as his interest in fiction declined, he renewed his interest in the events of his own life and undertook *A Son of the Middle Border* in 1911. When he had completed a revision in 1914, he was elated when Mark Sullivan, editor of *Collier's,* accepted six chapters for publication. The five sketches that appeared in *Collier's* in 1914 under the title *A Son of the Middle Border* were purportedly based upon an abandoned autobiographical manuscript by Lincoln Stewart (the hero of *Boy Life*).[10] Alternating between first-person accounts by Lincoln Stewart and third-person editorial comments by Garland, the five published sketches bring Garland to his early years at Cedar Valley Seminary. The first three relate the story of the move to Iowa and Garland's boyhood experiences in Wisconsin; the fourth deals with the period from 1869 to 1876, which also includes an account of his father's return from the Civil War; the fifth treats his experiences in Osage and concludes with a visit to the seminary.

Although the narrative technique is awkward, the *Collier's* installments anticipate the book-length version of *A Son of the Middle Border.* Unlike *Boy Life,* the accounts of such activities as haying, threshing, and cornhusking are condensed in order to expand the theme of the drudgery of farm work and to show Garland's growing rebellion against his farm life.

In 1914 Garland began the revision of *A Son of the Middle Border* to prepare it for book publication, and three installments of this revision appeared in *Collier's* from March to May, 1917.[11] In these first-person sketches—which are condensed versions of similar sections in the final book form—Garland takes us through the seminary to the eve of his departure for Boston in 1884.

IV   A Son of the Middle Border

A Son of the Middle Border is clearly the most successful of Garland's autobiographical works; and, with the possible exception of *Rose of Dutcher's Coolly,* it is also the most sophisticated of his longer works. Despite occasional sentimentalism, factual inaccuracies, and bothersome digressions, it remains one of the most carefully conceived, searching, and complex autobiographies in American literature. In it, Garland is able to blend several compelling themes which he had treated in one fashion or another in his other fiction; and he presents them in an intensely personal, lively, consuming narrative.

The narrative covers the period in Garland's life from 1865 to 1893. By telling the story of the Garlands and the McClintocks, the two sides of Garland's immediate family whose history reaches back to Scotland and forward to California, he was able to record a universal pioneer epic. For it is on one level a story about American nineteenth-century immigration and the moving frontier, the pioneer spirit and the gradual disillusionment of the pioneer ideal. Thus the book is, in one sense, a monument to the trials and hardships of "Westering."

However, the past to which Garland returns is more of a private one than that of a whole generation which he had presented in *Boy Life*. Garland emphasized that the subject was not so much the West, but the West as he had seen it. The account therefore takes the form of a personal history which chronicles the middle-border as a child might have experienced it and from which he escaped—only to remain attracted to it. All of the incidents are important for their effect on the narrator. Thus, while the movement of Garland's personal history is symbolic of the typical American during the last half of the nineteenth century, the force and richness of the work, as Donald Pizer suggests, stems from Garland's ability to combine an intensely personal theme of his family conflict with the objective reality of the setting in which it occurs, and to combine the personal with a larger cultural theme which emerges out of the setting.[12] Garland identifies the attitudes in his own youth with the pioneer spirit and his later ones in maturity with the decline of that spirit at the turn of the century.

The story opens simply from a child's perspective and foreshadows the major themes in the work:

All of this universe known to me in the year 1864 was bounded by the wooded hills of a little Wisconsin coulee, and its center was the cottage in which my mother was living alone—my father was in the war. As I project myself back into that mystical age, half lights cover most of the valley. The road before our doorstep begins and ends in vague obscurity—and Gramma Green's house at the fork of the trail stands on the very edge of the world in a sinister region peopled with bears and other menacing creatures. Beyond this point all is terror and darkness.[13]

Maintaining his point of view of a four-year-old, Garland relates the same incident used in "The Return of the Private"—the return of

his father from war—before shifting to a depiction of his grand-
parents, uncles, and aunts in relation to their frontier environment.

The conflict between Garland and his strict military disciplinarian father, who represents the pioneering spirit, and his
sympathy for his mother, who accepts the continued moves as well
as the drudgery and poverty of farm life with quiet resignation,
provides Garland with his principal theme. For more than anything
else, *A Son of the Middle Border* is about Garland's relationship
with his parents and how that relationship influenced his personal
development and eventual discovery as an artist. Although Garland
was excited by the idea of pioneering, he began to share his
mother's reluctance to move each time his father was determined to
uproot the family, first from Green's Coolly in 1888, then from their
farm in Minnesota to Mitchell County, Iowa, the following year,
finally to South Dakota in 1881. In 1876, when the family moved
temporarily to Osage, Iowa, where Garland's father worked as a
wheat buyer for the Grange, both Hamlin and his mother were
overjoyed with the prospect of being released from the hardships of
farm life. However, within a year, they were back on the farm.

His rebellion against his father, and all that he represented, finally climaxes when his father decided to pioneer once again and
Garland, asserting his individualism, struck out on his own for a
career in the East. However, while the rebellion against his father
was complete, he became increasingly bothered by feelings of guilt
at abandoning his mother, desiring to rescue her from her life of
misery. During one of his visits after he had been in Boston in 1887,
Garland was particularly struck with the oppressive conditions of
farm life:

In those few days I perceived life without its glamor. I no longer looked
upon these toiling women with the thoughtless eyes of youth. I saw no
humor in the bent forms and graying hair of the men. I began to understand that my own mother had trod a similar slavish round with never a full
day of leisure, with scarcely an hour of escape from the tugging hands of
children, and the need of mending and washing clothes. . . . the essential
tragedy and hopelessness of most human life under the conditions into
which society was swiftly hardening embittered me, called for expression,
but even then I did not know that I had found my theme. I had no intention at the moment of putting it into fiction.[14]

Thus the pattern of escape-guilt-return is established that is woven
throughout the narrative.

The realization of himself as a "son of the Middle Border" came only after this trip to the West and his meeting with Joseph Kirkland who convinced him that he must tell the story of the Middle Border. When Garland began to develop his themes for fiction, especially for the stories which comprised *Main-Travelled Roads*, the escape-guilt-return motif became central.

But Garland's rebellion against his father did not imply a rejection of the West. Indeed, Garland's relationship to the West as a son of a pioneer and as a writer were as important as his earlier rebellion. Garland characterized farm life as an unreconciled mixture of beauty and ugliness. Consequently, at one point, after a storm had ruined his family's crops, Garland could write that "My father's bitter revolt, his impotent fury appalled me, for it seemed to me (as to him), that nature was, at the moment, an enemy. . . . Most authors in writing of 'the merry, merry farmer' leave out experiences like this—they omit the mud and the dust and the grime, they forget the army worm, the flies, the heat, as well as the smells and drudgery of the barns. Milking cows is spoken of in the traditional fashion as a lovely pastoral recreation, when as a matter of fact it is a tedious job. We all hated it. We saw no poetry in it."[15] This passage is followed shortly by several pages that present a more romantic view:

Nothing could be more generous, more joyous, than these natural meadows in summer. The flash and ripple and glimmer of the tall sunflowers, the myraid voices of gleeful bobolinks, the churp and gurgle of red-winged blackbirds swaying on the willows, the meadow larks piping from grassy bogs, the peep of the prairie chicks and the wailing call of clover on the flowery green slopes of the uplands made it all an ecstatic world to me. It was a wide world with a big, big sky which gave alluring hint of the still more glorious unknown wilderness beyond.[16]

Such ambivalence is characteristic of Garland's view of the West and of the pioneer spirit. For not only could Garland be critical of his father's pioneer spirit, but he could also depict the decline of that spirit sympathetically and see in it the loss of his own youthful illusions.

While Garland evokes the pioneer spirit in both his father and in the McClintocks, the most pathetic figure in the book is Garland's uncle, David McClintock. Uncle David is first characterized as Garland's boyhood hero who plays the song on his violin that runs throughout the book as the families prepare to move on: "O'er the hills in legions, boys." But we later find Uncle David a beaten, exhausted, disillusioned pioneer in California. In one of the most poignant scenes in the book, Uncle David plays his fiddle for the last time at a family reunion in California; and Garland realizes how a once proud and strong man has been destroyed by the false hopes of the pioneer dream:

It was hard for me to adjust myself to his sorrowful decline into old age. I thought of him as he appeared to me when riding his threshing machine up the coulee road. I recalled the long rifle with which he used to carry off the prizes at the turkey shoots and especially I remembered him as he looked while playing the violin on that far off Thanksgiving night in Lewis Valley. . . . the David of my idolatry, the laughing giant of my boyhood world, could be found now, only in the mist which hung above the hills and valleys of Neshonoc.[17]

After Garland became an established writer in the East, he was still bothered by his desertion of his mother, but he claimed his final victory over his father by settling his weary and aged parents in a home in West Salem, Wisconsin, in 1893 before his father could again strike out for the West. *A Son of the Middle Border* closes with a Thanksgiving dinner in the new homestead in West Salem where Hamlin replaces his father at the head of the table and carves the turkey: "For the first time in my life I took position as head of the family and the significance of this fact did not escape the company. The pen had proved itself to be mightier than the plow. Going east had proved more profitable than going west!"[18]

With his final victory, Garland not only assuaged his guilt by rescuing his parents and by discovering himself as a writer but, ironically, realized that his self-discovery and success as a spokesman for the middle-border had emerged from his rejection of the West. In addition, he was able to evoke his sense of loss and to realize that he could never lose his emotional identification with the middle-border—an identification which was as strong as his rebellion against it.

V   *The Final Writings*

Of the three remaining autobiographies which complete the picture of Garland's chronicle, *A Daughter of the Middle Border* is one of his best, although all suffer by comparison with *A Son of the Middle Border*. Since the story resumes the family chronicle where *A Son of the Middle Border* ends, Garland depicts his marriage to

Zulime Taft, the "heroine" of the volume; the death of his mother; and the coming of his two daughters. The narrative closes with the death of his father and the beginning of World War I.

In *A Daughter of the Middle Border*, Garland's expressed intention was to provide a complement to *A Son of the Middle Border*. Since the action in *A Daughter* moves into the region of middle age, its theme becomes more personal, its scenes less epic. Garland considered this book a study of individuals and their relationships rather than of settlements and migrations.[19] Although the work lacks the charm and universal attraction of boyhood that was a central part of *A Son of the Middle Border*, it is significant as a record of Garland's intellectual development. Not only are we able to see the sources and circumstances of the composition of his principal romantic works, but we are better able to understand his psychological moods which were crucial in his artistic evolution. We get a keen insight into his attempt to cope with middle age; the exaltation which he experienced in the mountains, followed by the painful task of writing about it; and his disappointment and depression caused by the lack of critical acceptance.

Garland recognized that most of the moods and qualities which had given charm to *A Son of the Middle Border* were absent from the second volume, that the splendor of childhood and the heroism of pioneering could not be a constituent part of a narrative dealing with middle age. Furthermore, he knew that "in recording the decay of a masterful generation and the passing glory of the wilderness, I must chart an inevitable requiem, sorrowful and stern. The charm of youth was gone."[20]

Significantly less successful was *The Trail-Makers of the Middle Border*. Although not the first autobiography to be written, it is the first of the series in chronological order. It recounts the story of Richard Garland's migration from Maine to Boston and finally to Wisconsin in 1850 where he united with the McClintocks. The narrative closes in 1865, where Hamlin has his first recollections of his father. As the word "recollections" implies, Garland is dealing in this book with events which had been passed down to him. While he took some liberty with the facts and while he chose to change the real names of some of the major characters, the story was essentially factual. But it lacks most of those qualities which gave both *A Son of the Middle Border* and *A Daughter of the Middle Border* their richness.

Like *Trail-Makers From the Middle Border*, Garland's last

volume in the series, *Back-Trailers of the Middle Border,* suffers in comparision with the first two. Although structually it is carefully conceived and although it contains some of Garland's best writing, it lacks a sufficient theme to carry the narrative. In this volume Garland records the history of his family from the time of his father's death in 1914 to the present (1928). By recording the removal of his family to the East, which he characterized as a reversal of family progress, he attempted to show that "as the lives of Richard Garland, Isabelle Garland, Don Carlos Taft and Lucy Foster Taft embody the spirit of the pioneers so their grandchildren and my own later life illustrate the centripetal forces of the Nation. In taking the back-trail we are as typical of our time as our fathers were of theirs."[21]

As Garland became more and more absorbed with the past as he had remembered it, he dwelt in reminiscences. These reminiscences became the central part of his four volumes, *Roadside Meetings, Companions on the Trail, My Friendly Contemporaries,* and *Afternoon Neighbors.* Lacking the artistic merit of his earlier autobiographical volumes, they nevertheless provide interesting, although nostalgic, information regarding Garland's intellectual and artistic development.

For Garland the remembered past became, therefore, his reality. His final comments in *Back-Trailers from the Middle Border* serve as a fitting culmination of his distinguished, though erratic, artistic career:

Some say it is all an illusion, this world of memory, of imagination, but to me the remembered past is more and more a reality, a joyous secure reality. . . . Rejoicing in the mental law which softens outlines and heightens colors, I have written faithfully, in the hope of adding my small part to the ever-increasing wealth of our home-spun national history. When irritated by my surroundings and saddened by current comment, I have sought refuge in the valleys of my memory—an aging man's privilege. A few readers, each year becoming fewer, have encouraged me in this task and now it is ended. My story is told. I drop my pen and turn my face to the fire.[22]

CHAPTER 8

Conclusion

U LTIMATELY, we must recognize that Hamlin Garland was not an outstanding artist and that his significant works were the product of a brief span of time, despite the fact that he was writing fiction for over fifty years. However, we can also recognize that he was a capable writer who is often admired for his powerful, if uneven, style, for the vivid impressions he created, and for the moving and sensitive treatments of his themes. He could create pictures and scenes and capture feelings and attitudes in memorable ways. And he could elicit sympathetic responses to his situations and characters, gaining respect from readers and fellow writers consistently, despite the fact that he had difficulty sustaining his effects throughout his longer works. Garland's place in the literary history of the United States has been assured by literary historians because he carved a place in the historical development of the literature of the Middle West. He will be remembered largely for the fiction he wrote before 1895, which included his best work, *Main-Travelled Roads*, and for his autobiographical volumes, *A Son of the Middle Border, A Daughter of the Middle Border*, and *Roadside Meetings*.

Through his fiction, Garland became a principal spokesman for nineteenth-century agrarian society. In his best fiction, Garland illustrated that it had at last become possible to deal with the American farmer in literature as a human being rather than to see him simply through the veil of literary convention. By creating new types of characters, Garland hoped not only to inform readers of the harsh realities of Western farm life but to touch the deeper feelings of a nation.

While Garland was not "the first actual farmer in American fiction," as Joseph Kirkland proclaimed in 1887, he was the first of the realists to discover the prairie in stories which not only recognized the hardship, frustration, and sterility of farm life but also presented the glories of the open spaces and adventure on the plains. And he

114

was one of the first novelists to view skeptically the conventional American belief in the purity, wholesomeness, and freedom of life on the farm.

Faithful to his innate instinct for telling the truth, Garland used particular settings in the Midwest to bring to his readers the problems which men and women in crude surroundings had to face and solve in order to survive. He succeeded in reflecting the severe constriction of prairie life, with its loneliness and drudgery in the post - Civil-War decades, and suggested the waste of finer values exacted by life on the farm. He used the prairie for the setting because he knew it thoroughly from his own observation. In almost all of his commentary on his middle-border fiction, Garland emphasized that his view was that of a native: "I see life from the working side of the fence, and not from the buggy of the visiting city novelist. I was one of the men binding the grain under the scorching sun, and I was not noticing the glint and shimmer of the light on the golden grain. The beauty of the scene is there truly enough, but beneath it all are pain and squalor. I aim to put all there is in the scene, on the surface and beneath, into my pictures. The golden butter and sunshine do not make up the whole of farm life."[1]

Most readers acknowledge that Garland's finest work, *Main-Travelled Roads*, is an important historical document; for it portrays more vividly than any other work of its time the conditions which led to the Populist revolt. But it is also important for its artistic success. In praising the book William Dean Howells observed that "these stories are full of the bitter and burning dust, the foul and trampled slush, of the common avenues of life, the life of the men who hopelessly and cheerlessly make the wealth that enriches the alien and the idler, and impoverishes the producer."[2] Garland himself later recalled that he "put in the storm as well as the sun. I included the mud and manure as well as the wild roses and the clover."[3]

Despite Garland's weaknesses as a writer of fiction and the fact that several of the stories in *Main-Travelled Roads* are marred, the book as a whole is moving. By making the volume more than merely a collection of related stories, Garland was able to paint an absorbing picture of rural life in America. In *Main-Travelled Roads*, as elsewhere, Garland's strength lay in his ability to master situation and scenes rather than plot. While Garland's stories are informative,

they contain much more than mere reporting. In this regard
Thomas Bledsoe has observed that

it is narrative art of a rather high order built on careful and complex
arrangement which moves steadily toward the resolution. And this order
always directly serves the theme; Garland makes full use of his intimate
knowledge of midwestern life, but he never lets it get the better of him.
Unlike the reporter, he uses detail not merely to make what *happened*
vivid, but to flesh out a theme—the germ which moral indignation
planted—by incidents which may or may not have happened but un-
deniably could have. Unlike the tract writer, he is not concerned simply
with the moral; he develops his idea with the most credible realistic detail,
detail so rich it has a life and significance of its own.[4]

In addition to Garland's historical importance and his occasionally achieving notable results in his fiction of social protest and local
color, he is significant for another reason. While not an original
thinker, Garland reflected in his works the most vital intellectual,
social, and aesthetic ideas of his time, responding as a zealous
reformer to such issues as the rise of Populism, the single tax, Indian
rights, the struggle for women's rights, evolution, local color, and
impressionism.

With the publication of *Crumbling Idols* in 1894, Garland took
his place beside William Dean Howells as a spokesman for the new
currents that were forming in American literary history. Though he
was not to follow his own advice in his later romances, he
nevertheless indicated the direction that future writers would take.
Furthermore, Garland's autobiographical volumes, which chronicle
his acquaintence with innumerable writers, publishers, artists, and
politicians, are a rich record of the America of his day.

The direction that Garland's career took after 1895, when he was
producing his best and most honest work, remains one of the most
paradoxical in American letters. Ironically, his desire to write more
acceptable material in order to gain respectability seriously dam-
aged his art. Unfortunately, as we have seen, Garland was not often
able to integrate his social and literary theories with the materials
he gathered from personal experience and observation. Whenever
he was able to maintain a tension between his radical individualism
and the oppressive social and economic forces threatening individual freedom, his work retains a compelling vitality.

Notes and References

Chapter One

1. *A Son of the Middle Border* (New York, 1962), p. 270.
2. Ibid., p. 73.
3. Ibid., p. 273.
4. Donald Pizer, *Hamlin Garland's Early Work and Career* (New York, 1960), p. 6.
5. *Roadside Meetings* (New York, 1930), p. 8.
6. Ibid., p. 9.
7. Ibid., p. 13.
8. *Boston Evening Transcript*, May 16, 1887; quoted in Clyde E. Henson, *Joseph Kirkland* (New York, 1962), p. 93.
9. Henson, p. 93.
10. *A Son of the Middle Border*, p. 301.
11. Ibid., p. 310.
12. Ibid., p. 314.
13. Pizer, *Hamlin Garland's Early Work and Career*, p. 58.
14. Letters quoted in Pizer, *Hamlin Garland's Early Work and Career*, p. 68.
15. See Donald Pizer's "The Garland-Crane Relationship," *Huntington Library Quarterly* 24 (November, 1960), 75 - 82, which straightens out confusing dates.
16. *A Son of the Middle Border*, p. 372.
17. Ibid., p. 372.
18. *A Daughter of the Middle Border* (New York, 1923), p. 21.
19. See, for example, Bernard I. Duffey, "Hamlin Garland's Decline from Realism," *American Literature* 25 (March, 1953), 69 - 74; James D. Koerner, "Comment on 'Hamlin Garland's Decline from Realism,'" *American Literature* 26 (November, 1954), 427 - 32; and Claude Simpson, "Hamlin Garland's Decline," *Southwest Review* 26 (Winter, 1941), 223 - 34.
20. Pizer, *Hamlin Garland's Early Work and Career*, p. 2.
21. *A Daughter of the Middle Border*, p. 31.
22. Jean Holloway, *Hamlin Garland* (Austin, Texas, 1960), p. 133.
23. Ibid., p. 138 - 41.
24. *A Daughter of the Middle Border*, p. 42.
25. Holloway, *Hamlin Garland*, p. 146.
26. *Trail of the Goldseekers* (New York, 1899), p. 60.
27. Quoted in Holloway, p. 150.

28. *A Daughter of the Middle Border*, pp. 87 - 88.

29. Ibid., p. 89.

30. Holloway, p. 214.

31. Ibid., p. 242.

32. *Back-Trailers From the Middle Border* (New York, 1928), pp. 78 - 79.

33. H. L. Mencken, "A Stranger on Parnassus," in *Prejudices: First Series* (New York, 1919).

34. Henry B. Fuller, *Under the Skylights* (New York, 1901), p. 139.

Chapter Two

1. William Dean Howells, *Criticism and Fiction* (New York, 1891), p. 73.

2. Ibid., p. 128.

3. Herbert Spencer, *First Principles* (New York, 1885), p. 396. For Spencer's acceptance and application in America, see Richard Hofstadter, "The Vogue of Spencer," in *Social Darwinism in American Thought, 1860 - 1915* (Philadelphia, 1945), pp. 18 - 36.

4. In "Herbert Spencer and the Genesis of Hamlin Garland's Critical System," *Tulane Studies in English* 7 (1958), 153 - 68, Donald Pizer has argued convincingly that Garland found the development of local color compatible with Spencer's doctrine of progression. I am indebted to Pizer's chapter "The Development of a Literary Creed," in *Hamlin Garland's Early Work and Career*, probably the best treatment of the influences on Garland's critical theory.

5. The work was never published, but is extant in manuscript fragments, along with several unpublished lectures, in the Hamlin Garland Collection, University of Southern California Library. Extracts from Garland's lectures on "The Modern Novel" and "The Literature of Democracy," along with two lecture circulars for 1888 - 1889 and 1891, are printed in Lars Ahnebrink, *The Beginnings of Naturalism in American Fiction* (New York, 1961), pp. 440 - 50.

6. Pizer, *Hamlin Garland's Early Work and Career*, pp. 15 - 19.

7. *Crumbling Idols* (New York, 1894), p. 64.

8. Ibid., p. 22.

9. *A Son of the Middle Border*, p. 328.

10. *My Friendly Contemporaries* (New York, 1934), p. 131.

11. *Aesthetics*, trans. W. H. Armstrong (Philadelphia, 1879), p. xxii.

12. Ibid., p. 389.

13. Pizer, *Hamlin Garland's Early Work and Career*, pp. 22 - 23.

14. Howells, *Criticism and Fiction*, p. 145.

15. *Crumbling Idols*, p. viii.

16. Ibid., p. 35.

17. Quoted in Ahnebrink, pp. 139 - 40.

18. *Roadside Meetings*, pp. 252 - 53.

19. *Crumbling Idols*, p. 52.

Chapter Three

1. Pizer, *Hamlin Garland's Early Work and Career*, p. 31.

2. This story has been revived and analyzed by C. E. Schorer in "Hamlin Garland's First Published Story," *American Literature* 25 (March, 1953), 89 - 92. See also Garland's own account in *Roadside Meetings*, pp. 36 - 37.

3. *Belford's Magazine* 1 (July, 1888), 191 - 92.

4. See Donald Pizer, "John Boyle's Conclusion: An Unpublished Middle Border Story by Hamlin Garland," *American Literature* 31 (March, 1959), 59 - 75.

5. Ibid., p. 73.

6. Ibid., p. 62.

7. William Dean Howells, *Prefaces to Contemporaries 1882 - 1920*, ed. George Arms et al. (Gainesville, Fla., 1957), p. 38.

8. *Main-Travelled Roads* (Boston, 1891), "Preface." Quotations from the first edition all follow this edition. In subsequent editions Garland made a great many changes in the text of the original six stories besides adding new stories.

9. Mane, *Hamlin Garland: L'homme et l'oeuvre* (Paris, 1968), pp. 281 - 82.

10. *Main-Travelled Roads*, pp. 215 - 16.

11. Ibid., p. 74.

12. This theme is developed well by Thomas A. Bledsoe, "Introduction," in *Main-Travelled Roads* (New York, 1967).

13. *Main-Travelled Roads* (Boston, 1891), pp. 81 - 82.

14. Ibid., pp. 75 - 76.

15. Ibid., p. 82.

16. Ibid., p. 77.

17. Ibid., 126 - 27.

18. Pizer, "Introduction," in *Main-Travelled Roads* (Columbus, Ohio, 1970), p. xv.

19. *Main-Travelled Roads* (Boston, 1891), pp. 175 - 76.

20. Ibid., pp. 183 - 84.

21. Ibid., p. 260.

22. Holloway, *Hamlin Garland*, p. 290. Mane also disagrees with Pizer's contention that it has the same balance. He says, for example, that the Ripleys belong to another group even though they are prairie people. Garland eventually took out "Saturday Night on the Farm" and included it in *Boy Life on the Prairie* (chapter 12).

23. Pizer, *Hamlin Garland's Early Work and Career*, p. 76.

24. *Prairie Folks* (New York, 1899), p. 84.

Chapter Four

1. Anonymous article in the *Progressive Farmer* (Raleigh), April 28, 1887; quoted in John Hicks, *The Populist Revolt* (Minneapolis, 1931), p. 54. For the background of the Populist revolt, I am generally relying on Hick's study. Other important books dealing with this subject are Richard Hofstadter, *The Age of Reform* (New York, 1955); Norman Pollack, *The Populist Response to Industrial America* (New York, 1962); and Sylvia Bowman, *The Year 2000: A Critical Biography of Edward Bellamy* (New York, 1958).

2. Sylvia Bowman, *The Year 2000: A Critical Biography of Edward Bellamy*, pp. 123 - 34.

3. Ibid., p. 134.

4. Pizer, *Hamlin Garland's Early Work and Career*, pp. 95 - 96.

5. Ibid., p. 91.

6. *Roadside Meetings*, p. 126.

7. "The Single-Tax in Actual Operation" *The Arena* 10, (June, 1894), p. 57.

8. Walter Taylor, *The Economic Novel in America* (Chapel Hill, 1942), p. 156.

9. Pizer, *Hamlin Garland's Early Work and Career*, p. 97.

10. "Author's Preface," in *Under the Wheel, A Modern Play in Six Scenes* (Boston, 1890); quoted in Pizer, *Hamlin Garland's Early Work and Career*, p. 82.

11. *Jason Edwards, An Average Man* (Boston, 1892), pp. 24 - 25.

12. Ibid., p. 27.

13. Ibid., p. 42.

14. Ibid., p. 43.

15. Ibid., p. 139.

16. Ibid., p. 208.

17. Ibid., p. 182.

18. *My Friendly Contemporaries* (New York, 1932), p. 395.

19. Mane, *Hamlin Garland: L'homme et l'oeuvre*, p. 236.

20. The program of the play is published in Lars Ahnebrink, pp. 454 - 55.

21. For a discussion of these influences see Robert Mane, p. 243; Lars Ahnebrink, p. 363; and Donald Pizer, *Hamlin Garland's Early Work and Career*, pp. 84 - 85.

22. *A Member of the Third House: A Dramatic Story* (Chicago, 1892), p. 19.

23. Ibid., p. 48.

24. Ibid., p. 198.

25. Ibid., p. 42.

26. Mane, *Hamlin Garland: L'homme et l'oeuvre*, p. 247.

27. Ibid., p. 248.

28. Quoted in Lars Ahnebrink, p. 85.
29. *A Spoil of Office: A Story of the Modern West* (Boston, 1892), p. 192.
30. Ibid., p. 371.
31. Ibid., p. 294.

Chapter Five

1. Letter from Garland to Stone, January 18, 1894; referred to in Mane, p. 254.
2. Mane, *Hamlin Garland: L'homme et l'ouevre*, p. 257.
3. Pizer, *Hamlin Garland's Early Work and Career*, p. 103.
4. *The Moccasin Ranch* (New York, 1909), pp. 27 - 28.
5. Ibid., pp. 129 - 30.
6. Quoted by Donald Pizer in "Introduction" to *Rose of Dutcher's Cooly* (Lincoln, Neb., 1969), p. x. This edition is reproduced from the 1895 edition of *Rose* published by Stone and Kimball. Quotations from the novel are from this edition.
7. Pizer, "Introduction," in *Rose of Dutcher's Coolly*, p. xi.
8. Ibid., p. xvi.
9. Ahnebrink *The Beginnings of Naturalism in American Fiction*, p. 191.
10. *Stephen Crane: Letters*, ed. R. W. Stallman and Lillian Gilkes (New York, 1960), p. 14.
11. "An Ambitious French Novel and a Modest American Story," *Arena* 8 (June, 1893), xii.
12. It is significant, in this regard, that Garland, in order to satisfy his readers, who were offended by the term "sex-maniac," removed the phrase in his 1899 revised edition. In addition to several other revisions, Garland also added a section at the end of the 1899 edition making it absoluolutely clear that Rose and Mason are to be legally married, although that fact seemed obvious enough in the 1895 edition.
13. Letter from Garland to Floyd Logan, February 5, 1934; quoted in Ahnebrink, p. 205.
14. Letter from Garland to Carl Van Doren, March 2, 1920, which was not sent; quoted in Ahnebrink, p. 205 - 06, n.
15. *Rose of Dutcher's Coolly*, pp. 22 - 23.
16. Ibid., p. 23.
17. Ibid., pp. 31 - 32.
18. Ibid., p. 32.
19. Ibid., p. 116.
20. Mane, *Hamlin Garland: L'homme et l'oeuvre*, p. 268.
21. *Rose of Dutcher's Coolly*, p. 119.
22. Ibid., pp. 127 - 28.
23. Ibid., p. 182.
24. Ibid., p. 205.

25. Ibid., p. 380.

26. Chronologically, the stories previously appeared as follows: "Before the Low Green Door" ("A Common Case"), *Belford's Magazine* 1 (July, 1888), 188 - 99 and *Standard*, July 28, 1888, p. 6; "The Prisoned Soul" ("Under the Dome Capitol: A Prose Etching"), *Arena* 6 (September, 1892), 468 - 70; "At the Beginning" ("Before the Overture") *Ladies Home Journal* 10 (May, 1893), 13; "A Fair Exile" ("A Short-Term Exile"), *Literary Northwest* 3 (July, 1893), 303 - 15; "The Owner of the Mill Farm" ("A Graceless Husband"), *Northest Miller*, December, 1893, pp. 51 - 63; "An Alien in the Pines" ("Only a Lumberjack"), *Harper's Weekly* 38 (December 8, 1894), 1158 - 59; "A Preacher's Love Story" ("Evangel in Cyene"), *Harper's Monthly* 91 (August, 1895), 375 - 90; "A Meeting in the Foothills" (A Girl from Washington"), *Bacheller Syndicate*, January 16, 1896; "Upon Impulse" (same title), *Bookman* 4 (January, 1897), 428 - 32; "A Stop-over at Tyre" ("A Girl of Modern Tyre"), *Century*, n.s. 21 (July, 1897), 401 - 43. "A Sheltered One," "The Passing Stranger," and "The End of Love is Love of Love," all found their first appearance in *Wayside Courtships*.

27. *Wayside Courtships* (New York, 1897), pp. 280 - 81.

28. Ibid., pp. 165 - 66.

29. Ibid., p. 167.

30. Ibid., p. 169.

Chapter Six

1. *A Daughter of the Middle Border*, p. 21.

2. Ibid., pp. 28 - 29.

3. Ibid., p. 31.

4. Ibid., p. 52.

5. *The Eagle's Heart* (New York, 1900), p. 3.

6. Ibid., p. 220.

7. Ibid., p. 9.

8. Ibid., p. 14.

9. Ibid., p. 143.

10. Ibid., p. 18.

11. Mane, *Hamlin Garland: L'homme et l'oeuvre*, p. 311.

12. *Her Mountain Lover* (New York, 1901), p. 133.

13. Ibid., p. 192.

14. Holloway, *Hamlin Garland*, p. 158.

15. See the Selected Bibliography for the history of the publication of the stories collected in *They of the High Trails*.

16. "Author's Foreword," in *They of the High Trails* (New York, 1916).

17. Holloway, *Hamlin Garland*, p. 229.

18. *They of the High Trails*, pp. 91 - 92.

19. Roy Harvey Pearce, *The Savages of America* (Baltimore, 1953),

p. 58. See also Pearce's "The Significance of the Captivity Narrative," *American Literature* 19 (March, 1947), 1 - 20.

20. Quoted in Pearce's *The Savages of America*, p. 63.

21. Nicholas Karolides, *The Pioneer in the American Novel* (Norman, Oklahoma, 1967), briefly develops these three trends.

22. See Gregory L. Paine, "The Indians of the Leatherstocking Tales," *Studies in Philology* 23 (1926), 16 - 39; Albert Keiser, *The Indian in American Literature* (New York, 1933), pp. 101 - 43; and Kay Semour House, *Cooper's Americans* (Columbus, Ohio, 1965).

23. *A Daughter of the Middle Border*, pp. 248 - 49.

24. James K. Folsom, *The American Western Novel* (New Haven, Conn., 1966), p. 149.

25. *The Book of the American Indian* (New York, 1923), pp. 1 - 2.

26. Ibid., p. 4.

27. Ibid., p. 7.

28. Ibid., p. 63.

29. Ibid., p. 30.

30. Ibid., p. 139.

31. Ibid., pp. 152 - 53.

32. Folsom, *The American Western Novel*, p. 155.

33. *The Book of the American Indian*, p. 170.

34. Ibid., p. 205.

35. Ibid., pp. 209 - 10.

36. Ibid., pp. 273 - 74.

37. *The Captain of the Gray-Horse Troop* (New York, 1902), p. 126.

38. Quoted in Mane, p. 354.

39. *Hesper* (New York, 1903), p. 387.

40. *Companions on the Trail* (New York, 1931), pp. 311 - 12.

41. Letter from W. D. Howells to Garland, November 3, 1903 (Garland Papers, University of Southern California).

Chapter Seven

1. Holloway, *Hamlin Garland*, p. 214.

2. "Boy-Life on the Prairie," *American Magazine* 7 (January, 1888), 299 - 303; (March, 1888), 570 - 77; (April, 1888), 684 - 90; 8 (June, 1888), 148 - 55; (July, 1888), 296 - 302; (October, 1888), 712 - 17.

3. Donald Pizer, "Hamlin Garland's *A Son of the Middle Border:* Autobiography as Art," in *Essays in American and English Presented to B. R. McElderry, Jr.*, ed. Max L. Schultz (Athens, Ohio, 1967), p. 78.

4. "Boy Life on the Prairie" (New York, 1899), p. vi.

5. This preface is reprinted in *Boy Life on the Prairie* (Lincoln, Nebraska, 1961), p. 426 - 27. For convenient reference, all quotations from the text itself are taken from this edition, which is a reprint of the 1899 Macmillan edition.

6. "Introduction," in *Boy Life on the Prairie,* p. vi.

7. *Boy Life on the Prairie,* p. 418.

8. Ibid., pp. 412 - 15.

9. Pizer, "Hamlin Garland's *A Son of the Middle Border:* Autobiography as Art," p. 81.

10. *Collier's* 53 (March 28, 1914), 5 - 7, 22 - 23; (April 18, 1914), 11 - 12, 21 - 22, 24 - 25; (May 9, 1914), 15 - 16, 25 - 26, 28 - 30; (June 27, 1914), 13 - 14, 31 - 33; (August 8, 1914), 20 - 21, 31 - 32. The sixth sketch, "Golden Days at Cedar Valley Seminary," did not appear at this time because the series was interrupted by the outbreak of World War I. It finally did appear in 1917: March 31, pp. 9 - 10; April 21, pp. 8 - 9; May 26, pp. 13 - 14. In this sketch Lincoln Stewart was dropped entirely.

11. *Collier's* 56 (March 31, 1917), 9 - 10, 25 - 26, 28 - 30; (April 21, 1917), 8 - 9, 27, 30; (May 26, 1917), 13 - 14, 49.

12. Pizer, "Hamlin Garland's *A Son of the Middle Border:* Autobiography as Art," p. 91.

13. *A Son of the Middle Border,* p. 1.

14. Ibid., p. 310.

15. Ibid., p. 109.

16. Ibid., p. 112 - 13.

17. Ibid., pp. 384 - 85.

18. Ibid., p. 394.

19. *A Daughter of the Middle Border,* p. xi.

20. *Back-Trailers From the Middle Border* (New York, 1928), p. 143.

21. Ibid., p. viii.

22. Ibid., p. 378.

Chapter Eight

1. Quoted in Pizer, *Hamlin Garland's Early Work and Career,* p. 164.

2. Howells, *Prefaces to Contemporaries 1822 - 1920,* p. 38.

3. *Roadside Meetings,* p. 179.

4. Thomas Bledsoe, "Introduction," in *Main-Travelled Roads* (New York, 1954), p. xxxii.

Selected Bibliography

PRIMARY SOURCES

1. Manuscripts
The chief collection of unpublished manuscripts, in the Doheny Library of the University of Southern California, Los Angeles, includes notebooks, letters, diaries, and marginalia. The Garland-Gilder correspondence is in the New York Public Library.

2. Books
Main-Travelled Roads. Boston: Arena Publishing Company, 1891. Fiction.
Jason Edwards. Boston: Arena Publishing Company, 1892. Fiction.
A Member of the Third House. Chicago: A. J. Shulte, 1892. Fiction.
A Little Norsk: Ol' Pap's Flaxen. New York: D. Appleton, 1892. Fiction.
Prairie Songs. Cambridge: Stone & Kimball, 1893. Poetry.
Prairie Folks. Cambridge: Stone & Kimball, 1893. Fiction.
Crumbling Idols: Twelve Essays on Art. Chicago: Stone & Kimball, 1894. Collection of Essays.
Rose of Dutcher's Coolly. Chicago: Stone & Kimball, 1895. Fiction.
Wayside Courtships. New York: D. Appleton, 1897. Fiction.
The Spirit of Sweetwater. New York: Doubleday & McClure, 1898. Fiction.
Ulysses S. Grant: His Life and Character. New York: Doubleday & McClure, 1898. Biography.
Boy Life on the Prairie. New York: Macmillan, 1899. Fiction.
The Trail of the Goldseekers. New York: Macmillan, 1899. Fiction.
The Eagle's Heart. New York: D. Appleton, 1900. Fiction.
Her Mountain Lover. New York: Century Company, 1901. Fiction.
The Captain of the Gray-Horse Troop. New York: Harper & Brothers, 1902. Fiction.
Hesper. New York: Harper & Brothers, 1903. Fiction.
The Light of the Star. New York: Harper & Brothers, 1904. Fiction.
The Tyranny of the Dark. New York: Harper & Brothers, 1905. Fiction.
Witch's Gold. New York: Doubleday & Page, 1906. Fiction.
Money Magic. New York: Harper & Brothers, 1907. Fiction.
The Long Trail. New York: Harper & Brothers, 1907. Fiction.
The Shadow World. New York: Harper & Brothers, 1908. Fiction.
Moccasin Ranch: A Story of Dakota. New York: Harper & Brothers, 1909. Fiction.
Cavanaugh: Forest Ranger. New York: Harper & Brothers, 1910. Fiction.
Other Main-Travelled Roads. New York: Harper & Brothers, 1910. Fiction.

Victor Ollnee's Discipline. New York: Harper & Brothers, 1911. Fiction.
The Forester's Daughter. New York: Harper & Brothers, 1914. Fiction.
They of the High Trails. New York: Harper & Brothers, 1916. Fiction.
A Son of the Middle Border. New York: Macmillan, 1917.
A Daughter of the Middle Border. New York: Macmillan, 1921. Autobiography.
A Pioneer Mother. Chicago: The Bookfellows, 1922. Autobiography.
The Book of the American Indian. New York: Harper & Brothers, 1923. Fiction.
Trail-Makers of the Middle Border. New York: Macmillan, 1926. Autobiography.
The Westward March of American Settlement. Chicago: American Library Association, 1927. Critical essays.
Back-Trailers from the Middle Border. New York: Macmillan & Company, 1928. Autobiography.
Prairie Song and Western Story. New York: Allyn and Bacon, 1928. Fiction.
Roadside Meetings. New York: Macmillan, 1930. Autobiography.
Companions on the Trail. New York: Macmillan, 1931. Autobiography.
My Friendly Contemporaries. New York: Macmillan, 1932. Autobiography.
Afternoon Neighbors. New York: Macmillan, 1934. Autobiography.
Iowa, O Iowa. Iowa City: Clio Press, 1935. Fiction.
Joys of the Trail. Chicago: The Bookfellows, 1935. Fiction.
The Long Trail [containing "The Return of the Private"]. New York: Harper & Brothers, 1935. Fiction.
Forty Years of Psychic Research. New York: Macmillan, 1936. Autobiography.
The Mystery of the Buried Crosses. New York: E. P. Dutton, 1939. Fiction.

3. Articles

"Carlyle as a Poet." *Boston Evening Transcript*, August 2, 1887, p. 5.
"Boy Life on the Prairie." *American* 7 (January, 1888), 299 - 303; (March, 1888), 570 - 77; (April, 1888), 684 - 90; 8 (June, 1888), 296 - 302; (October, 1888), 712 - 17.
"Land at Ten Cents an Acre." *Boston Evening Transcript*, January 12, 1888, p. 6.
"Hunger for Land." *Boston Evening Transcript*, January 30, 1888, p. 6.
"Professor Garland's Western Trip." *Standard*, June 23, 1888, p. 3.
"In Minneapolis." *Standard*, July 28, 1888, p. 2.
"American Novels." *Literary News* 9 (August, 1888), 236 - 37.
"Work in New Fields." *Standard*, August 25, 1888, p. 8.
"Cheering Words from Professor Garland." *Standard*, November 7, 1888, p. 3.
"For Club Houses at Small Expense." *Standard*, January 12, 1889, p. 2.
"The Tragedy of a Town." *Boston Evening Transcript*, April 6, 1889, p. 10.
"Hints for a Spring and Summer Campaign in Massachusetts." *Standard*, April 13, 1889, p. 13.

"The Greek Play." *Boston Evening Transcript,* May 1, 1889, p. 2.

"The Cause of Poverty." *Dawn* 1 (June 15, 1889), 1 - 2.

"Whitman at Seventy, How the Good Gray Poet Looks and Talks." *New York Herald,* June 30, 1889, p. 7.

"In New Hampshire." *Standard,* August 24, 1889, p. 5.

"An Interesting Announcement." *Standard,* September 28, 1889, p. 3.

"Herbert Spencer on Property." *Standard, October* 12, 1889, p. 6.

"Mr. Howells's Latest Novels." *New England Magazine* 2 (May, 1890), 243 - 50.

"The Massachusetts Plan." *Standard,* May 7, 1890, p. 12.

"Ibsen as a Dramatist." *Arena* 2 (June, 1890), 72 - 82. Reprinted in *Crumbling Idols.*

"Women and their Organization." *Standard,* October 8, 1890, pp. 5 - 6.

"A New Declaration of Rights." *Arena* 3 (January, 1891), 157 - 84.

"The Future of 'The Standard.' " *Standard,* August 26, 1891, p. 9.

"Mr. and Mrs. Herne." *Arena* 4 (October, 1891), 543 - 60.

"Mr. Howells's Plans." *Boston Evening Transcript,* January 1, 1892, p. 6.

"The Alliance Wedge in Congress." *Arena* 5 (March, 1892), 447 - 57.

"Sprigs of Lilac for Walt Whitman." *Conservation* 3 (June, 1892), p. 26.

"Psychography: Mr. Garland's Report." *Psychical Review* 1 (August, 1892), 43 - 44.

"Salt Water Day." *Cosmopolitan* 13 (August, 1892), 387 - 94.

"An Experiment in Psychography." *Psychical Review* 1 (November, 1892), 136 - 37.

"The West in Literature." *Arena* 6 (November, 1892), 669 - 76. Reprinted in *Crumbling Idols.*

"Sounds, Voice, and Physical Disturbances in the Presence of a Psychic." *Psychical Review* 1 (February, 1893), 226 - 29.

"The Future of Fiction." *Arena* 7 (April, 1893), 513 - 24. Reprinted in *Crumbling Idols.*

"Real Conversations—II. A Dialogue Between Eugene Field and Hamlin Garland. Recorded by Hamlin Garland." *McClure's* 1 (August, 1893), 195 - 204.

"Literary Emancipation of the West." *Forum* 16 (October, 1893), 156 - 166. Reprinted in *Crumbling Idols.*

"Report of Dark Seances, with a Non-Professional Psychic, For Voices and the Movement of Objects Without Contact." *Psychical Review* 2 (November, 1893 - February, 1894), 152 - 177. Written in conjunction with T. E. Allen and B. O. Flower.

"A Pioneer Christmas." *Ladies Home Journal* 11 (December, 1893), 11.

"Western Landscapes." *Atlantic Monthly* 72 (December, 1893), 805 - 9.

"The Land Question, and its Relation to Art and Literature." *Arena* 9 (January, 1894), 165 - 75.

"Boy Life in the West—Winter." *Midland Monthly* 1 (February, 1894), 113 - 22.

"Real Conversations—IV. A Dialogue Between James Whitcomb Riley and

Hamlin Garland. Recorded by Mr. Garland." *McClure's* 2 (February, 1894), 219 - 34.

"Homestead and Its Perilous Trades. Impressions of a Visit." *McClure's* 3 (June, 1894), 3 - 20.

"The Single Tax in Actual Application." *Arena* 10 (June, 1894), 52 - 58.

"An American Tolstoi. Hamlin Garland Describes a Visit to Joaquin Miller's Farm." *Philadelphia Press*, June, 17, 1894, p. 26.

"Productive Conditions of American Literature." *Forum* 17 (August, 1894), 690 - 98.

"Mount Shasta." *Midland Monthly* 2 (December, 1894), 481 - 83.

"A Night Landing on the Mississippi River." *Midland Monthly* 3 (February, 1895), 142 - 43.

"My Grandmother of Pioneer Days." *Ladies' Home Journal* 12 (April, 1895), 10.

"Whitman and Chicago University." *Conservator* 6 (June, 1895), 60 - 61.

"Work of an Art-Association in Western Towns." *Forum* 19 (July, 1895), 606 - 9.

"Torture of Branding." *Chicago Daily News*, October 2, 1895, p. 9.

"Art Conditions in Chicago." *Chicago Art Institute*, 1895, pp. 5 - 8.

"Into the Happy Hunting Grounds of the Utes." *Harper's Weekly* 40 (April 11, 1896), 350 - 51. Syndicated by the Albert Bigelow Paine Syndicate.

"Among the Moki Indians." *Harper's Weekly* 11 (August 15, 1896), 801 - 7. Albert Bigelow Paine Syndicate.

"The Most Mysterious People in America." *Ladies' Home Journal*, October, 1896, pp. 5 - 6. Alibert Bigelow Paine Syndicate.

"The Whole Troop was Water Drunk." Bacheller Syndicate, November 7, 1896.

"A Stern Fight with Cold and Hunger." Bacheller Syndicate, November 16, 1896.

"With the Silver Miner; Hard Luck Story of the Small Prospector." Syndicated by the McClure Syndicate, 1896.

"With the Placer Miners; A Glimpse of Cripple Creek in 1896." Syndicated by the McClure Syndicate, 1896.

"In the Klondike; The Grim Realities of the Overland Trail." *Cleveland Leader*, July 31, 1896.

"A Hard Citizen and His Side of It." Syndicated by the McClure Syndicate, 1896.

"The Early Life of Ulysses S. Grant." *McClure's* 8 (December, 1896), 125.

"Grant at West Point." *McClure's* 8 (January, 1897), 195 - 210.

"Grant in the Mexican War." *McClure's* 8 (February, 1897), 366 - 80.

"Grant's Quiet Years at Northern Posts." *McClure's* 8 (March, 1897), 402 - 12.

"Grant's Life in Missouri." *McClure's* 8 (April, 1897), 514 - 20.

"Grant at the Outbreak of War." *McClure's* 9 (May, 1897), 601 - 10.

"Grant's First Great Work in the War." *McClure's* 9 (June, 1897), 721 - 26.

"Grant in a Great Campaign." *McClure's* 9 (July, 1897), 805 - 11.

"Grant, His First Meeting with Lincoln." *McClure's* 9 (August, 1897), 892.

"Ho for the Klondike." *McClure's* 10 (March, 1898), 443 - 54.

"The Grant and Ward Failures." *McClure's* 10 (April, 1898), 498 - 505.

"Ulysses S. Grant, His Last Year." *McClure's* 11 (May, 1898), 86 - 96.

"General Custer's Last Fight as Seen by Two Moon." *McClure's* 11 (September, 1898), 443 - 48.

"Hitting the Trail." *McClure's* 12 (January, 1899), 298 - 304; *University Record* (University of Chicago) 10 (1905), 53 - 56. Also published as "Vanishing Trails."

"I. Zangwill." *Conservative Review* 2 (November, 1899), 402 - 12.

"Impressions of Paris in Times of Turmoil." *Outlook* 63 (December 16, 1899), 968 - 73.

"Prairie Route to the Golden River." *Independent* 51 (January 26, 1900), 241 - 51.

"Tramps on the Trail." *Cosmopolitan* 26 (March, 1900), 12.

"Stephen Crane: A Soldier of Fortune." *The Saturday Evening Post* 183 (July 28, 1900), 16 - 17.

"Herne's Sincerity as a Playwright." *Arena* 25 (September, 1901), 282 - 84.

"Delmar of Pima." *McClure's* 17 (February, 1902), 340 - 48.

"The Redman's Present Needs." *North American Review* 174 (April, 1902), 476 - 88.

"Automobiling in the West." *Harper's Weekly* 46 (September 6, 1902), 1254.

"Will the Novel Disappear?" *North American Review* 175 (September, 1902), 289 - 96.

"Culture or Creative Genius." *Outlook*, December 6, 1902, pp. 780 - 91.

"The Work of Frank Norris." *Critic* 42 (March, 1903), 216 - 18.

"Sanity in Fiction." *North American Review* 176 (March, 1903), 3336 - 48.

"The Red Man as Material." *Booklover's Magazine* 2 (August, 1903), 196 - 98.

"Building a Fireplace in Time for Christmas." *Country Life in America* 8 (October, 1905), 645 - 47.

"The Shadow World." *Everybody's Magazine* 8 - 9 (April - October, 1908).

"Shadow World Prize Winners." *Everybody's Magazine* 9 (November, 1908), 665 - 79.

"Ernest Howard Crosby and His Message." *Twentieth Century Magazine* 1 (October, 1909), 27 - 28.

"My Aim in Cavanagh." *World's Work*, October, 1910, pp. 1356 - 59.

" 'Starring' the Play." *Nation* 92 (July 20, 1911), 54.

"My First Christmas Tree." *Ladies' Home Journal* 28 (December, 1911), 13.

"Local Color as the Vital Element of American Fiction." *Proceedings of the American Academy of Arts and Letters*, 4 (December, 1911), 41 - 45.

"Middle West—Heart of the Country." *Country Life* 22 (September 15, 1912), 19 - 24, 44.

"Poet of the Sierras." *Sunset* 30 (June, 1913), 765 - 70.

"Must Men Always be Beasts, Trampling Women in the Mire?" *Cleveland Press*, June 4, 1913.

"The New Chicago." *Craftsman* 24 (September, 1913), 555 - 65.

"Stephen Crane as I Knew Him." *Yale Review* 3 (April 1, 1914), 494 - 506.

"On the Road with James A. Herne." *Century* 88 (August, 1914), 574 - 81.

"Meetings with Howells." *Bookman* 45 (March, 1917), 1 - 7.

"William Dean Howells: Master Craftsman." *Art World* 1 (April, 1917), 411 - 12.

"Graven Image." *Art World* 2 (May, 1917), 126 - 30.

"A Word about Bacheller." *American* 85 (April, 1918). 19.

"The Crime of Profiteering." *Colorado Springs Gazette*, September 24, 1918, p. 4.

"Reading Aloud to the Child." *Kindergarten Primary Magazine* 31 (January, 1919), 134.

"My Neighbor Theodore Roosevelt." *Everybody's Magazine* 41 (October, 1919), 9 - 16, 94.

"Going to School in Iowa." *Education Review* 54 (December, 1919), 435 - 39.

"The Coming of Sir Oliver Lodge." *Touchstone* 6 (January, 1920), 217.

"Theodore Roosevelt." *Mentor* 7 (February 2, 1920), 1 - 12.

"The Spirit World on Trial." *McClure's* 52 (March, 1920), 33 - 34.

"William Dean Howells's Boston: A Posthumous Pilgrimage." *Boston Transcript*, May 22, 1920.

"Ulysses S. Grant." *Mentor* 8 (July, 1920), 1 - 11.

"A Great American" [Howells]. *New York Evening Post, Literary Review*, March 5, 1921, pp. 1 - 2.

"Westward Migrations." *New York Times*, August 14, 1921, p. 8.

"My Friend John Burroughs." *Century* 102 (September, 1921), 731 - 42.

"Midwestern Sculptor: The Art of Lorado Taft." *Mentor* 11 (October, 1923), 19 - 24.

"The American Academy of Arts and Letters." *Bookman* 63 (November, 1923), 89 - 92.

"Pioneers and City Dwellers." *Bookman* 58 (December, 1923), 369 - 72.

"Introduction." In *The Autobiography of David Crockett*, pp. 3 - 10. New York: Charles Scribner's Sons, 1923.

"The Limitations of Authorship in America." *Bookman* 54 (May, 1924), 257 - 61.

"Roosevelt as Historian." In *The Winning of the West*, III, ix - xvii. New York: Charles Scribner's Sons, 1924.

"Memories of Henry George." *Libertarian* 5 (November, 1925), 280.

"The White Weasel." *Dearborn Independent* 27 (December 18, 1926), 4, 5, 27.

"John Burroughs." *World Review* 4 (June 16, 1927), 265.

"Doris Ullman's Photographs." *Mentor* 15 (July, 1927), 42 - 44.

"The Dark Side of the Moon." *Dearborn Independent,* July 2, 1927, pp. 3, 18, 19.

"Recollections of Roosevelt." In *Roosevelt As We Knew Him,* edited by E. S. Wood. Philadelphia: John C. Winston Company, 1927.

"I Don't Know What Happened at these Seances." *American* 105 (March, 1928), pp. 42 - 43, 142 - 48.

"Songs and Shrines of Old New England." *Current Literature* 6 (March 25 - 29, 1929), 38 - 40.

"Roadside Meetings of a Literary Nomad." *Bookman* 70 - 71 (October, 1929 - July, 1930).

"The Value of Melodious Speech." *Emerson Quarterly* 9 (November, 1929), 5, 6, 22.

"Fortunate Coast." *Saturday Evening Post* 202 (April 5, 1930), 31.

"Books of my Childhood." *Saturday Review* 7 (November 15, 1930), 347.

"Some of my Youthful Enthusiasms." *English Journal,* May, 1931, pp. 555 - 62.

"How I Got My Literary Start." *Scholastic Magazine,* June, 1931, p. 355.

"The Westward March of Settlement." *Frontier Times* 12 (August, 1935), 499 - 505.

"A Man Most Favored." *Mark Twain Quarterly* 1 (Summer, 1937), 3.

"Homage to the Pioneers." *Stepladder* 23 (September, 1937), 162 - 63.

"We Go Up the Hill." *Stepladder* 23 (December, 1937), 218 - 19.

"Two Excellent Bookmen." *Stepladder* 24 (January, 1938), 3.

"Literary Fashions Old and New." *Think* 4 (March, 1939), 14, 24, 27.

"Let the Sunshine In." *Rotarian* 55 (October, 1939), 8 - 11.

"Quiet Acceptance." *Mark Twain Quarterly* 3 (Spring, 1940), 11.

"Dan Beard and the Scouts." *Mark Twain Quarterly* 4 (Summer, 1940), 12.

"Twain's Social Conscience." *Mark Twain Quarterly* 4 (Summer, 1940), 13.

4. Book Reviews

"The Moonlight Boy." *Boston Evening Transcript,* July 16, 1886, p. 6. Review of the novel by E. W. Howe.

"Lemuel Barker." *Boston Evening Transcript,* January 31, 1887, p. 6. Review of W. D. Howells' *The Minister's Charge.*

"Bret Harte's New Book." *Boston Evening Transcript,* February 3, 1887, p. 6. Review of *A Millionaire of Rough-and-Ready* by Bret Harte.

"Confessions of Claude." *Boston Evening Transcript,* May 4, 1887, p. 6. Review of the novel by Edgar Fawcett.

"Zury: The Meanest Man in Spring County." *Boston Evening Transcript,* May 16, 1887, p. 3. Review of the novel by Joseph Kirkland.

"Seth's Brother's Wife." *Boston Evening Transcript,* November 11, 1887, p. 6. Review of the novel by Harold Frederic.

"April Hopes." *Boston Evening Transcript,* March 1, 1888, p. 6. Review of the novel by W. D. Howells.

"High Ground." *Boston Evening Transcript,* March 21, 1888, p. 6. Review of the book by Augustus Jacobson.

"A Man Story." *Boston Evening Transcript*, November 7, 1888, p. 6. Review of the novel by E. W. Howe.

"Whitman's 'November Boughs.'" *Boston Evening Transcript*, November 1888, p. 6.

"Annie Kilburn." *Boston Evening Transcript*, December 27, 1888, p. 6. Review of the novel by W. D. Howells.

"Mr. Howells's Latest Novel." *Boston Evening Transcript*, December 14, 1889, p. 10. Review of *A Hazard of New Fortunes*.

"Mark Twain's Latest." *Boston Evening Transcript*, January 10, 1890, p. 6. Review of *A Connecticut Yankee*.

"A Great Book." *Standard*, February 5, 1890, pp. 5 - 6. Review of W. D. Howells's *A Hazard of New Fortunes*.

"Mr. Herne's New Play." *Boston Evening Transcript*, July 8, 1890, p. 6. Review of *Margaret Fleming*.

"Canada and the Gold Question." *Arena* 4 (August, 1891), xxiv. Review of the book by Goldwin Smith.

"The Silver Question." *Arena* 4 (August, 1891), xxv. Review of *Silver in Europe* by S. Dana Horton.

"A Plea for Liberty." *Arena* 4 (September, 1891), xvii - xxiv. Review of a collection of essays.

"Wallace's 'National Selection.'" *Arena* 4 (October, 1891), xxv - xxviii. Review of the book by Alfred R. Wallace.

"Mr. George's Work on Free Trade." *Arena* 4 (November, 1891), xlii - xliii. Review of Henry George's *Protection and Free Trade*.

"Two New Novels." *Arena* 5 (December, 1891), xxxvi - xxxviii. Review of Ignatius Donnelly's *Dr. Huguet* and Joseph Kirkland's *The Captain of Company K*.

"Matter, Ether and Motion." *Arena* 6 (October, 1892), 1. Review of the book by Amos E. Dolbear.

"Onoqua." *Arena* 6 (October, 1892), 1 - 1i. Review of the novel by Frances E. Sparhawk.

"Opie Read's Novels." *Arena* 6 (October, 1892), xlix. Review of *Emmett Benlore*.

"Who Pays Your Taxes?" *Arena* 6 (November, 1892), lxxi - lxxii. Review of a collection of essays.

"On the Oregon Trail." *Bookbuyer* 9 (December, 1892), 500 - 503. Review of a new edition of the book by Francis Parkman.

"An Ambitious French Novel and a Modest American Story." *Arena* 8 (June, 1893), xi - xii. Review of Paul Bourget's *Cosmopolis* and Stephen Crane's *Maggie*.

"Washington Brown, Farmer." *Arena* 8 (September, 1893), xxiii. Review of the novel by Leroy Armstrong.

"Co-Operative Banking." *Arena* 8 (October, 1893), xv. Review of the book by W. H. Van Ornum.

"Money Found." *Arena* 8 (November, 1893), xv - xvi. Review of the book by Thomas E. Hill.

"In Re Walt Whitman." *Arena* 9 (January, 1894), i - ii. Review of the book edited by Horace L. Traubel.

"Henry George's Last Book." *McClure's* 10 (February, 1898), 396. Review of *A Perplexed Philosopher*.

"Outlines in Local Color." *Bookbuyer* 4 (January, 1898), 690 - 92. Review of the book by J. B. Matthews.

5. Plays

"Under the Wheel: A Modern Play in Six Scenes." *Arena* 2 (July, 1890), 182 - 228. Reprinted as *Under the Wheel* (1890).

6. Poems

"Edwin Booth." *Boston Evening Transcript*, January 2, 1886, p. 7.

"Logan at Peach Tree Creek." *Boston Evening Transcript*, January 1, 1887, p. 6. Reprinted in *Prairie Songs*.

"Prairie Memories." *American* 6 (October, 1887), 653. Reprinted in *Prairie Songs*.

"Beneath the Pines." *American* 7 (November, 1887), 87. Reprinted in *Prairie Songs*.

"My Cabin." *American* 7 (December, 1887), 232. Reprinted in *Prairie Songs*.

"Lost in the Norther." *Harper's Weekly* 31 (December 3, 1887), 883. Reprinted in *Prairie Songs*.

"The Coming Storm." *Boston Evening Transcript*, March 28, 1888, p. 6.

"Paid His Way." *America* 1 (May 19, 1888), 6. Reprinted in *Prairie Songs*.

"A Wind from the East Sea." *Standard*, March 9, 1889, p. 11.

"Apology." *Literary World* 20 (June 8, 1889), 192. Reprinted in *Prairie Songs*.

"Points of View." *Standard*, June 22, 1889, p. 15.

"A Dakota Wheat-Field." *Youth's Companion* 62 (July 18, 1889), 366. Reprinted in *Prairie Songs*.

"The Average Man." *America* 2 (July 25, 1889), 526.

"By the River." *Youth's Companion* 62 (August 15, 1889), 410. Reprinted in *Prairie Songs*.

"Scepterless Kings." *Standard*, August 17, 1889, p. 9.

"Single Tax Cat." *Standard*, September 7, 1889, p. 14.

"Music Land: At a Symphony." *New England Magazine*, n.s. 3 (January, 1891), 628 - 30.

"In Winter Night." *Literary Northwest* 2 (December, 1892), 96. Reprinted in *Prairie Folks*.

"A Ridge of Corn." *Harper's Weekly* 37 (August 12, 1893), 763. Reprinted in *Prairie Songs*.

"O Cool Gray Jug!" *Harper's Weekly* 37 (August 19, 1893), 786. Reprinted in *Prairie Songs*.

"A Summer Mood." *New England Magazine*, n.s. 9 (September, 1893), 64. Reprinted in *Prairie Songs*.

"Prairie Fires." *Youth's Companion* 66 (September 14, 1893), 444. Reprinted in *Prairie Songs*.
"Sport." *New England Magazine*, n.s. 9 (October, 1893), 240. Reprinted in *Prairie Songs*.
"Prairie Chickens." *Independent* 45 (October 5, 1893), 1329. Reprinted in *Prairie Songs*.
"The Cry of the Artist." *Chap-Book* 4 (November 15, 1895), 7 - 8.
"The Magic Spring." *The Cliff-Dwellers' Yearbook* (Chicago) (1911), p. 37.
"The Trail Makers." *Twentieth Century Magazine* 5 (December 1911), 156 - 58.
"The Lure of the Bugle." *Current Opinion* 61 (September, 1916), 199 - 200.
"Adventurous Boyhood." *Frontier Times* 12 (August, 1935), 503.
"Plowman of Today." *Rotarian* 4 (September, 1939), 6.

7. Short Fiction
"Ten Years Dead." *Every Other Saturday* 2 (March 28, 1885), 97 - 99.
"Holding Down a Claim in a Blizzard." *Harper's Weekly* 32 (January 28, 1888), 66 - 67.
"A Common Case." *Belford's* 1 (July, 1888), 188 - 99. Reprinted as "Before the Low Green Door" in *Wayside Courtships*.
"Mrs. Ripley's Trip." *Harper's Weekly* 32 (November 24, 1888), 894 - 95. Reprinted in *Main-Travelled Roads*.
"Under the Lion's Paw." *Harper's Weekly* 33 (September 7, 1889), 726 - 27. Reprinted in *Main-Travelled Roads*.
"Old Sid's Christmas." *Harper's Weekly* 33 (December 28, 1889), 1038 - 40.
"Drifting Crane." *Harper's Weekly* 34 (May 31, 1890), 421 - 22. Reprinted in *Prairie Folks*.
"Among the Corn-Rows." *Harper's Weekly* 34 (June 28, 1890), 506 - 8. Reprinted in *Main-Travelled Roads*.
"The Return of A Private." *Arena* 3 (December, 1890), 97 - 113. Reprinted in *Main-Travelled Roads*.
"The Test of Elder Pill." *Arena* 3 (March, 1891), 480 - 501. Reprinted in *Prairie Folks*.
"A Spring Romance." *Century* 42 (June, 1891), 296 - 302. Reprinted as "Wiliam Bacon's Hired Man" in *Prairie Folks*.
"A Prairie Heroine." *Arena* 4 (July, 1891), 223 - 46. Reprinted as "Sim Burn's Wife" in *Prairie Folks*.
"An Evening at the Corner Grocery: A Western Character Sketch." *Arena* 4 (September, 1891), 504 - 12. Reprinted as "Village Cronies" in *Prairie Folks*.
"Uncle Ripley's Speculation." *Arena* 5 (December, 1891), 125 - 35. Reprinted as "Uncle Ethan's Speculation" in *Prairie Folks*.
"A Spoil of Office: A Story of the Modern West." *Arena* 5 (January - May,

1892), 253 - 68, 376 - 400, 495 - 522, 619 - 44, 749 - 74; 6 (June, 1892), 104 - 32.

"Ol' Pap's Flaxen." *Century* 43 (March - April, 1892), 743 - 51, 912 - 23; 44 (May, 1892), 39 - 47. Reprinted in *A Little Norsk.*

"A Queer Case." *Youth's Companion* 65 (March 3, 10, 17, 1892), 105 - 6, 212 - 22, 133 - 34.

"Daddy Deering." *Belford's* 8 (April, 1892), 152 - 61. Reprinted in *Prairie Folks.*

"At the Brewery." *Cosmopolitan* 13 (May, 1892), 34 - 42. Reprinted as "Saturday Night on the Farm" in *Prairie Folks.*

"Under the Dome of the Capitol: A Prose Etching." *Arena* 6 (September, 1892), 468 - 70. Reprinted as "The Prisoned Soul" in *Wayside Courtships.*

"Forgetting." *Ladies' Home Journal* 10 (December 1892), 17. Reprinted as "The End of Love . . ." in *Wayside Courtships.*

"Before the Overture." *Ladies' Home Journal* 10 (May, 1893), 13. Reprinted as "At the Beginning" in *Wayside Courtships.*

"A Short-Term Exile." *Literary Northwest* 3 (July, 1893), 308 - 15. Reprinted as "A Fair Exile" in *Wayside Courtships.*

"A Graceless Husband." *Northwestern Miller,* Extra Christmas Number (December, 1893), 57 - 62. Reprinted as "The Owner of the Mill Farm" in *Wayside Courtships.*

"God's Ravens." *Harper's Monthly* 89 (June, 1894), 142 - 48. Reprinted in *Main-Travelled Roads.*

"Old Mosinee Tom." *New York Press,* November 4, 1894, pt. 4, p. 4. Syndicated by the Bacheller Syndicate.

"A Lynching in Mosinee." *New York Press,* November 11, 1894, pt. 5, p. 4. Syndicated by the Bacheller Syndicate.

"The Land of the Straddle-Bug." *Chap-Book* 2 (November 14, 1895), 5 - 11, 73 - 76, 134 - 42, 182 - 89, 223 - 29, 261 - 71, 304 - 19. Reprinted in *The Moccasin Ranch.*

"A Woman in the Camp: A Christmas Sketch." *Arena* 11 (December, 1894), 90 - 97.

"Only a Lumber Jack." *Harper's Weekly* 38 (December 8, 1894), 1158 - 59. Reprinted as "An Alien in the Pines" in *Wayside Courtships.*

"The Wapseypinnicon Tiger. A Pioneer Sketch." *Philadelphia Press,* February 28, 1895, p. 11; March 1, 1895, p. 11. Syndicated by the Bacheller Syndicate. Reprinted in *Prairie Folks.*

"An Evangel in Cyene." *Harper's Monthly* 91 (August, 1895), 375 - 90. Reprinted as "A Preacher's Love Story" in *Wayside Courtships.*

"A Grim Experience." *Philadelphia Press,* August 24, 1895, p. 9; Syndicated by the Bacheller Syndicate.

"Grace . . . A Reminiscence." *Philadelphia Press,* October 17, 1895, p. 11. Syndicated by the Bacheller Syndicate. Reprinted as "A Day of Grace" in *Prairie Folks.*

"Opposites." *Bookman* 2 (November, 1895), 196 - 97. Reprinted as "A Sheltered One" in *Wayside Courtships*.

"A Girl from Washington." Syndicated by the Bacheller Syndicate, January 16, 1896. Reprinted as "A Meeting in the Foothills" in *Wayside Courtships*.

"Captain Hance." Syndicated by the Bacheller Syndicate, October 27, 1896.

"A Division in the Coule." Syndicated by the Bacheller Syndicate, November 1, 1896. Reprinted as "Aidgewise Feelin's" in *Prairie Folks*.

"A Girl of Modern Tyre." *Century* 58 (January, 1897), 401 - 23. Reprinted as "A Stop-Over at Tyre" in *Wayside Courtships*.

"The Spirit of Sweetwater." *Ladies' Home Journal* 14 (August - October, 1897).

"Joe the Navajo Teamster." *Youth's Companion* 57 (November 18, 1897), 579 - 80.

"The Story of Buff." *Youth's Companion* 71 (December 2, 1897), 606 - 7.

"The Creamery Man of Molasses Gap." *Outlook* 57 (December 4, 1897), 838 - 45. Reprinted as "The Creamery Man" in *Main-Travelled Roads*.

"The Stony Knoll." *Youth's Companion* 71 (December 18, 1897), 635.

"Upon Impulse." *Bookman* 4 (January, 1897), 428 - 32. Reprinted in *Wayside Courtships*.

"The Doctor." *Ladies' Home Journal* (March, 1897 - March, 1898).

"A Good Fellow's Wife." *Century* 55 (April, 1898), 937 - 52. Reprinted in *Main-Travelled Roads*.

"Sam Markham's Wife." *Ladies' Home Journal* 15 (July, 1898), 8. Reprinted as "A Day's Pleasure in *Main-Travelled Roads*.

"Rising Wolf-Ghost Dancers." *McClure's* 12 (January, 1899), 241 - 48. Reprinted in *The Book of the American Indian*.

"The Man at the Gate of the Mountains." *Ladies' Home Journal* 16 (August, 1899), 9 - 10.

"The Electric Lady." *Cosmopolitan* 20 (May, 1900), 73 - 83.

"The Eagle's Heart." *The Saturday Evening Post* 172 - 173 (June 16 - September 8, 1900).

"Big Moggasen." *Independent* 52 (November 1, 1900), 2622 - 24. Reprinted in *The Book of the American Indian*.

"People of the Buffalo." *McClure's* 16 (December, 1900), 153 - 59; Reprinted as "The Storm Child" in *The Book of the American Indian*.

"Jim Matteson of Wagon Wheel Gap." *Century* 61 (November, 1900 - April, 1901). Reprinted in *Her Mountain Lover*.

"Bad Medicine Man." *Independent* 52 (December 6, 1900), 2899 - 904.

"The Drummer Boy's Alarm." *The Saturday Evening Post* 173 (March 9, 1901), 7.

"Homeward Bound." *Living Age* 129 (June, 1901), 594 - 96. Reprinted in *Her Mountain Lover*.

"A Tale of a Tenderfoot." *The Saturday Evening Post* 174 (August 24, 1901), 8 - 9.

"The Captain of the Gray-Horse Troop." *The Saturday Evening Post* 174 (December 14, 1901 - March 29, 1902).

"The River's Warning." *Frank Leslie's* 53 (January, 1902), 297 - 304. Reprinted in *The Book of the American Indian*.

"The Steadfast Widow Delaney." *The Saturday Evening Post* 174 (June 14, 28, 1902), 14, 28 Reprinted as "The Grub-Staker" in *They of the High Trails*.

"Hippy the Dare Devil." *McClure's* 19 (September 1902), 474 - 80.

"Sitting Bull's Defiance." *McClure's* 20 (November, 1902), 35 - 40.

"New Medicine House." *Harper's Weekly* 45 (December 6, 1902), 35 - 37. Reprinted in *The Book of the American Indian*.

"Nistina." *Harper's Weekly* 47 (April 4, 1903), 544 - 45. Reprinted in *The Book of the American Indian*.

"Lone Wolf's Old Guard." *Harper's Weekly* 47 (May 2, 1903), 716 - 18.

"The Faith of his Fathers." *Harper's Weekly* 47 (May 30, 1903), 892 - 93.

"The Outlaw." *Harper's Weekly* 47 (June 13, 1903), 927 - 73. Reprinted in *They of the High Trails*.

"The Iron Khiva." *Harper's Weekly* 47 (August 29, 1903), 1416 - 19. Reprinted in *The Book of the American Indian*.

"The Wife of a Pioneer." *Ladies' Home Journal* 20 (September, 1903), 8, 42. Reprinted in *A Pioneer Mother*

"The Light of the Star." *Ladies' Home Journal* 21 (January - May, 1903).

"Little Squatters." *Youth's Companion* 78 (June 9, 23, 1904).

"Two Stories of Oklahoma." *Century* 68 (June, 1904), 328 - 29.

"The Marshall's Capture." *Harper's Weekly* 48 (December 19, 1904), 34 - 40.

"The Tyranny of the Dark." *Harper's Weekly* 49 (January 28 - May 13, 1905).

"A Spartan Mother." *Ladies' Home Journal* 22 (February, 1905), 10 - 50. Reprinted in *The Book of the American Indian*.

"The Doctor's Visit." *Pall Mall Magazine* 35 (May, 1905), 558 - 90.

"Mart Haney's Mate." [Chapters 1 - 4]. *The Saturday Evening Post* 178 (November 18, 1905), 1 - 3, 27 - 32. Reprinted in *Money Magic*.

"The Fireplace." *Delineator* 66 (December, 1905), 1051 - 56, 1140 - 42. Reprinted in *Main-Travelled Roads*.

"The Long Trail: A Story of the Klondike." *Youth's Companion* 80 - 81 (December 6, 1906 - February 7, 1907).

"The Noose: A Story of Love and the Alien." *The Saturday Evening Post* 177 (June 6, 1906), 3 - 5, 18.

"In That Far Land." *Circle* 2 (October - November, 1907), 204 - 5, 298 - 300.

"Red Plowman." *Craftsman* 13 (November, 1907), 180 - 82.

"Money Magic." *Harper's Weekly* 11 (August 7 - October 12, 1907).

"The Healer of Mogalyon." *Circle*, March, 1908, 140 - 45.

"The Outlaw and the Girl." *Ladies' Home Journal* 25 (May - July, 1908). Reprinted as "The Outlaw" in *They of the High Trails.*

"A Night Raid at Eagle's River." *Century* 76 (September, 1908), 725 - 34. Reprinted as "The Cow-boss" in *They of the High Trails.*

"Nugget." *Sunset* 30 (April, 1913), 335 - 42.

"Kelly Afoot." *Sunset* 31 (November, 1913), 919 - 26. Reprinted as "The Trail Tramp" in *They of the High Trails.*

"Partners for a Day" *Collier's*, LII (March 14, 1914), 5 - 6. *They of the High Trails* ("The Trail Tramp").

"A Son of the Middle Border: A Personal History." *Collier's* 53: I, "Half Lights" (March 28, 1914), 5 - 7, 22 - 23; II, "Following The Sunset" (April 18, 1914), 11 - 12, 21 - 22, 24 - 25; III, "Woods and Prairie Lands" (May 9, 1914), 15 - 16, 26, 28 - 30; IV, "The Passing of the Prairie" (June 27, 1914), 13 - 14, 31 - 32; V, "Lincoln Enters Hostile Territory" (September 8, 1914), 20 - 21, 31 - 32.

"Kelly of Brimstone Basin." *National Sunday Magazine*, March 28, 1915, pp. 387 - 88, 392 - 94. Reprinted as "The Trail Tramp" in *They of the High Trails.*

"The Ranger and the Woman." *Collier's* 55 (August 24 - 28, 1915).

"A Son of the Middle Border." *Collier's* 59: "Golden Days at Cedar Valley Seminary" (March 31, 1917), 9 - 10, 25 - 26; (April 21, 1917), 8 - 9, 27 - 30; "A Prairie Outpost" (May 26, 1917), 13 - 14, 49.

SECONDARY SOURCES

AHNEBRINK, LARS. *The Beginnings of Naturalism in American Fiction.* Cambridge, Mass.: Harvard University Press, 1950. Pp. 63 - 89 and passim. An exhaustive study of European influences on American novelists, including Garland.

BLEDSOE, THOMAS. Introduction. In *Main-Travelled Roads,* pp. ix - xliii. New York: Rinehart, 1954. Examines background, major themes, and form of *Main-Travelled Roads.*

DUFFY, BERNARD I. "Hamlin Garland's 'Decline' from Realism." *American Literature* 25 (March, 1953), 69 - 74. Examines Garland's Boston years (1884 - 1893); suggests that he was more concerned with success than reform.

FOLSOM, JAMES K. *The American Western Novel.* New Haven, Conn.: College and University Press, 1966. Pp. 149 - 55, 180 - 84, and passim. Provocative treatment of Garland's Indian material.

GRONEWOLD, BENJAMIN F. "The Social Criticism of Hamlin Garland." Ph.D. dissertation, New York University, 1943. Good investigation of Garland's social commentary.

HENSON, CLYDE E. "Joseph Kirkland's Influence on Hamlin Garland." *American Literature* 23 (January, 1952), 458 - 63. Examines the Kirkland-Garland correspondence.

HILL, ELDON C. "A Biographical Study of Hamlin Garland from 1860 to 1895." Ph.D. dissertation, Ohio State University, 1940. Pioneer biographical study of Garland.

HOLLOWAY, JEAN. *Hamlin Garland: A Biography.* Austin: University of Texas Press, 1956. Presents a thorough chronology of the genesis and composition of Garland's works.

KEISER, ALBERT. *The Indian in American Literature.* New York: Oxford University Press, 1933. Pp. 279 - 92 and passim. Presents background and examines themes of Garland's Indian material.

KOERNER, JAMES D. "Comment on 'Hamlin Garland's "Decline" from Realism.'" *American Literature* 26 (November, 1954), 427 - 32. Response to Duffy's articles.

MANE, ROBERT. *Hamlin Garland: L'homme et l'oeuvre (1860 - 1940).* Paris: Didier, 1968. The best comprehensive analysis of Garland's life and works.

McCULLOUGH, JOSEPH B. "Hamlin Garland's Quarrel with *The Dial.*" *American Literary Realism* 9 (Winter, 1976), 77 - 80. Reprints letters between Garland and Francis F. Browne, editor of *The Dial.* Letters, along with introduction, shed light on Garland's views on the function of literature and on the role of literary critics.

———. "Hamlin Garland's Letters to James Whitcomb Riley." *American Literary Realism* 9 (Summer, 1976), 249 - 60. Reprints letters from Garland to Riley, principally dealing with the question of dialect in American poetry and local color in fiction.

McELDERRY, BRUCE R., JR. Introduction. In *Boy Life on the Prairie.* Lincoln: University of Nebraska Press, 1961. Useful relative to several aspects of the novel.

PIZER, DONALD. "Hamlin Garland's *A Son of the Middle Border:* Autobiography as Art." In *Essays in American and English Literature Presented to B. R. McElderry, Jr.,* edited by Max L. Schultz, pp. 76 - 107. Athens: Ohio University Press, 1967. Examines the composition, themes, and form of the book.

———. *Hamlin Garland's Early Work and Career.* Berkeley: University of California Press, 1960. The best examination of Hamlin Garland's life and works between 1884 and 1895.

———. "Herbert Spencer and the Genesis of Hamlin Garland's Critical System." *Tulane Studies in English* 7 (1957), 153 - 68. Examines Garland's selective use of Spencer.

———. Introduction. In *Rose of Dutcher's Coolly.* Columbus, Ohio: Charles E. Merrill, 1969. A good examination of most aspects of the novel.

————. "Romantic Individualism in Garland, Norris and Crane." *American Quarterly* 10 (Winter, 1958), 463 - 75. Shows how these writers not only exhibit a naturalistic strain, but also a romantic individualistic strain going back to Thomas Jefferson and the transcendentalists.

————. "The Garland-Crane Relationship." *Huntington Library Quarterly* 24 (November, 1960), 75 - 82. Resolves many problems surrounding this relationship.

————. "The Radical Drama in Boston, 1889 - 1891." *New England Quarterly* 31 (September, 1958), 361 - 74. Good article for understanding Garland's involvement with drama, as well as influences on his radical thought.

SAUM, LEWIS O. "Hamlin Garland and Reform." *South Dakota Review* 10 (Winter, 1972 - 1973), 36 - 62. Examines Garland's reform impulse, as seen in his writing.

SIMPSON, CLAUDE. "Hamlin Garland's Decline." *Southwest Review* 26 (Winter, 1941), 223 - 34. Attempts to account for Garland's "decline" from realism.

TAYLOR, WALTER F. *The Economic Novel in America.* Chapel Hill, N.C.: University of North Carolina Press, 1942. Pp. 148 - 83. Contains a good chapter on Garland's social and economic commentary and importance.

WALCUTT, CHARLES C. *American Literary Naturalism, A Divided Stream.* Minneapolis: University of Minnesota Press, 1956. Pp. 53 - 63. Sees Garland as an early naturalist; investigates the determinism and protest in his works.

Index

(The works of Garland are listed under his name)

141

DATE DUE
